LIFE STORY OF A TRANSPLANTED MAN

A Memoir

VALLABH DHUDSHIA

LIFE STORY OF A TRANSPLANTED MAN
A MEMOIR

iUniverse books may be ordered through booksellers or by contacting:

iUniverse
1663 Liberty Drive
Bloomington, IN 47403
www.iuniverse.com
844-349-9409

ISBN: 978-1-6632-5188-6 (sc)
ISBN: 978-1-6632-5346-0 (hc)
ISBN: 978-1-6632-5187-9 (e)

Library of Congress Control Number: 2023905103

Print information available on the last page.

iUniverse rev. date: 06/30/2023

This memoir is dedicated to my life partner, Manju; my daughter, Neha; my son, Neel, and daughter-in-law, Charlotte; my grandchildren Austin, Abigail, and Cooper; and future generations to come.

CONTENTS

PREFACE

When we dig out a mature tree and transplant it to a new location, we do not know what will happen to it. Will it reestablish its roots at the new location? Will it adjust to the new soil and ecosystem? Will it grow, bloom, and bear fruits at the transplanted location?

Similarly, when you remove a mature man from his culture, society, environment, business systems, or living style, and transplant him to a new location, where all these things are different from what he was used to while growing up, will he survive the shock of the transplantation and thrive at the transplanted location?

I see millions of men and women who have been transplanted into the promised land of America (like I was). Some of them made it to the top of society, and some didn't. Every one of them has a sensational story of their life. This memoir is about my life story, about an ordinary man who was uprooted at the age of twenty-four from his culture, society, environment, business systems, living style, and diet, and was transplanted into a location where those things were different. It describes my life before and after the transplantation. It also describes how an ordinary and elementary school-educated farmer's son, living a very primitive life in a small village in India, gets an education, comes to America, gets further education, and becomes a successful professional who uplifts his family's living standards and raises two successful children who are now physicians.

The prime objective of writing this memoir is to leave something behind for my grandchildren and generations to come. I want them to know their roots and their ancestor who came to America. From where did he come to America? How much did he struggle to establish roots and thrive in America?

The other two objectives for writing this memoir are:

(i) to provide a road map for newly transplanted people, coming into the promised land of America, on how to establish roots in America and thrive. I have used the road map, and it worked superbly for me. It is especially more relevant to transplanted men and women from India.

(ii) to provide a guideline and format for those who want to write his/her own life stories.

The material presented in this memoir is based on:

(i) my personal diary and notes
(ii) whatever I heard from my elders
(iii) whatever I showed, understood, remembered, and experienced during my life so far

A few inaccuracies may have sneaked in unintentionally.

This memoir about my life cannot be told without including my life partner Manju's contribution to my life. I am grateful to her for being a part of my life. Her contributions make this story a mix of my story and ours.

I am grateful to my elders who shared their memories with me. Specifically, I am grateful to my brother, Devraj, for collecting, compiling, and presenting information about our family roots, family tree, and the history of my hometown, Shapur. I am also grateful to all my relatives, friends, teachers and professors, employers, managers and supervisors, and colleagues whose names I have referred to in this memoir.

Finally, I am also grateful to the iUniverse staff for editorial and publishing support for this memoir.

—Vallabh H. Dhudshia, PhD

1

FOREFATHERS

1.1 PROUD ROOTS

I was born and raised in a Kadwa Patidar (also known as Kadwa Kanabi or Kadwa Patel) Hindu family living in a small village called Shapur, in Gujarat, India. My family roots go all the way to the origin of Hindus. There are many theories about the origin of Hindus. Based on available historical records and credible evidence, the most realistic approach indicates that all Hindus came to India in 1500 BC from the Pamir region on the Ayu River in central Asia (in Azerbaijan) via the Caucasus Mountains and Afghanistan, as shown in the map below. At that time, they were called Aryans, and not Hindus. Their religion was not called Hinduism. At that time, they worshipped controlling natural forces like the sun, moon, wind, fire, water, rain, etc. They believed in one god, Brahman, and their religion was known as Sanatan dharma, Aryan dharma, or Vedic dharma. They rode horses and invented chariots. They used the swastika (卐) as a symbol of divinity and spirituality.

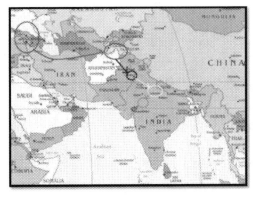

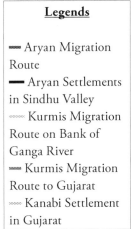

Legends

▬ Aryan Migration Route

▬ Aryan Settlements in Sindhu Valley

⋯ Kurmis Migration Route on Bank of Ganga River

▬ Kurmis Migration Route to Gujarat

⋯ Kanabi Settlement in Gujarat

Figure 1.1: Migration route of Aryans, Hindus, and Patidars.

The Aryans spoke a highly developed language, which is referred to as Proto-Indo-European (PIE). The PIE is the mother of Sanskrit, Latin, and most European languages. Sanskrit is the language of most Hindu scriptures. It is also the mother of most North Indian languages, including Hindi, Gujarati, Marathi, Bengali, Punjabi, etc.

When they came to India, they settled on the plains of a big river, which they named Sindhu (which means "big like the ocean"). With time, Aryans got mixed with natives living there. They accepted each other's social customs, equipment, animals, religion, gods, and goddesses. They established a well-organized settlement, which became known as the Saptasindhu (Sindhu) Valley civilization. Later, that area became known as the Punjab area (currently, some part is in India and some in Pakistan). While they were in the Sindhu Valley, they established trade with Mesopotamia, a historical region of Western Asia situated within the Tigris-Euphrates river system, in the northern part of the Fertile Crescent. In terms of the modern nation-state, it corresponds with much of Iraq, Kuwait, the eastern parts of Syria, southeastern Turkey, and regions along the Turkish-Syrian and Iran-Iraq borders and Iran. Those people cannot pronounce the sound of "s"; instead, they say the sound of "h." They started referring to the people of the Sindhu Valley as Hindu. This is how Aryans became Hindus.

When the Aryans came to India, the Aryan society was casteless. With time, the Aryan society settled in the Sindhu Valley, and it got divided into four social groups/classes, called *varna*. Varna is not the caste, but it represents a group of people with common temperamental characteristics. A person's varna is determined by his/her Karma (deeds), and not by birth (caste). As such, a person is free to choose his/her varna. However, with time, it became rigid.

Initially, there were four varnas (social groups/classes), as described below:

1. Brahmins: those who provided education and religious services
2. Kshatriya: those who protected (during wars) and ruled society
3. Vaishya: those who conducted business and commerce
4. Shudra: those who did manual work and served the other three groups

Later, the Kshatriya class got divided into three subclasses: Rajan Kshatriya (kings and leaders), Kshatriya (warriors), and Kurmi Kshatriya. The Kurmi Kshatriya farmed during peacetime and helped the army during times of war. Later, they became known only as Kurmis, working on farms growing food and raising milking cows for the benefit of the entire society.

Foreign invaders forced the Kurmis and others to leave the Punjab area around AD 1000.

When the Kurmis migrated from Punjab, those Kurmis who lived in the Karad area of Punjab became Kadwa Kurmi, and those who lived in the Leu area became Leuva Kurmis. With the time and migration to the south, the word Kurmi got distorted to Kanabi. Thus, Kadwa Kurmis became Kadwa Kanabi, and Leuva Kurmis became Leuva Kanabi. The word Kanabi means farmer.

Around AD 1700, all the Kurmis were renamed Patidars, which means "farming landowners." At that time, the Kurmis were the landowners. This renaming changed Kadwa Kurmis to Kadwa Patidars, and Leuva Kurmis to Leuva Patidars. Subsequently, the word Patidar got shortened to Patel. However, the word Patidar is still an extremely popular and frequently used word for Kurmis/Kanabi.

The hierarchy chart below shows an overview of the evolution of my roots. As shown in the chart, my early ancestors were Aryan in central Asia, then became Hindus, later became Kshatriya, and then Kurmis Kshatriya, Kurmi, Kadwa Kurmi, Kadwa Kanabi, Kadwa Patidar/Patel, and finally, remained Hindu.

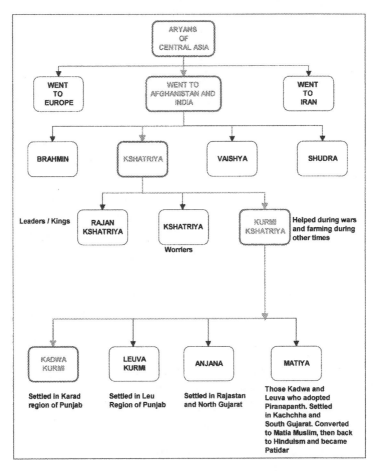

Figure 1.2: Evolution of Kadwa Patidars.

Due to frequent attacks from foreigners, the Patidar people were forced to move from Punjab and settled all over India. A few groups settled in the state of Gujarat and continued farming occupation.

Kadwa Patidars' different last names are related to the name of the original town in Punjab where they came from. My ancestors must have come from the town of Dholu, and they were called Dhuleshia. The last name got distorted in local dialects and English spelling. Last names such as Dhulesia, Dhuleshia, Dhulesiya, Dhudshia, Dhudasiya, Dhudashia, and Dhudasia are from the same family root.

Interestingly, my last name, Dhudshia, means "earthworm."

A. Patidars/Patels Transformation: Farmers to Mainstream Society

In the late eighteenth and early nineteenth centuries, most Patidars/Patels were hardworking, poor farmers living in small villages, with very little or no education. Most of the small villages didn't have a middle school and/or high school; therefore, Patidars/Patels didn't get an education to compete and fit in, mainstream society. As a result, they were left behind in society's hierarchy. Gradually some Patidars/Patels got some education and left the laborious farming occupation and went to other high-paying occupations and jobs. Once they settled down in the upper echelon of society, they started noticing that their relatives were still left behind, working very hard on farms and earning very little money. Those Patidars/Patels who made it to the upper echelon started encouraging those who had been left behind to get an education. When significant numbers of Patidars/Patels made it to the upper echelon of society, they developed plans to uplift the entire Patidar/Patel community by: (i) getting rid of those customs that were holding the Patidar/Patel community back, (ii) encouraging education by opening up subsidized and low-cost, boarding houses (dorms) for those Patidar/Patel students who neither had middle school nor high school in their village, and (iii) giving scholarships and interest-free loans for college education.

These initiatives started paying off in the 1950s, 1960, and 1970s. Those Patidars/Patels who got an education in their chosen field started leaving farming and becoming doctors, engineers, lawyers, teachers, accountants, small and large business owners, and high-level government officials. That transformed the entire landscape of Indian society, especially in the state of Gujarat. Patidars/Patels became an integral part the mainstream society.

I am one of those beneficiaries of the Patidar/Patel transformation.

B. Patidars/Patels Migration out of Gujarat

Many Patidar/Patels from Gujarat started migrating to Africa and the UK, but not to America, in the early nineteenth century. In the early 1950s, a few Patidars/Patels came to America. Most of them came as students for advanced degrees. They stayed in America after their education and settled in various professions. A big wave of Patidars/Patels came to America in the early 1960s, including me. Most of them came on student visas and got advanced degrees in engineering. They also stayed in America and settled in various professions. Some of them started exploring other businesses. In the late 1960s, America adopted a new immigration policy to attract highly educated people from all over the world. Many Patidars/Patels took advantage of the liberal visa policy and came to America on permanent visas (green cards). The biggest wave of Patidars/Patels came to America in the early 1970s when America adopted the family reunification visa policy. Under this policy, any American citizen (American-born or naturalized) can sponsor his/her spouse, child, parent, and siblings for an American permanent residency visa. This policy flooded America with Patidars/Patels. Many came without a college education. They explored various businesses. Many of them got into small- to midsize motels/hotels and convenience stores with gas station businesses. With their hardworking DNA, they became successful. Eventually, they monopolized these sectors of American businesses. At the same time, the first American-born generation of Patidars/Patels got into the mainstream of American professional businesses including medicine, engineering, business management, accounting, law, etc.

Recently, Gujaratis started migrating to Australia and New Zealand, too.

When I look back at history, I feel proud of my roots. Their evolution from Aryans to Hindus, to Kurmis, and then to Patidars is an enchanting journey that traverses through many countries with their highs and lows. They have impacted the cultures and economies of those places. In return, the places my ancestors lived in have shaped their characters. Throughout this journey, a few things have remained unchanged, like their hardworking nature, positive attitude, insistence on truth, cooperative nature, an inclination for helping other people, and a strong sense of brotherhood within the community. These very characteristics resulted in the affluence and rise of the Patidar/Patel communities in India, Africa, the UK, and America.

1.2 COURAGEOUS AND UNYIELDING GRANDPARENTS

A. Paternal Great-Grandfather: Devasi Dhudshia (1799–1870)

On my father's side, my great-grandfather, Devasi, was a well-known farmer in Vanthali, a midsize town, with sizable land and a good reputation in the local community. He lived an extremely basic, simple, and honest life. He never went to school. He was a fighter for justice and a proponent of social reforms. He was adventurous and forward-thinking. He was a staunch devotee of the Vaishnava sect of Hinduism. He defended it against the other Hindu sects. He did the pilgrimage, on foot, of northern India for three years, during which he visited all the Hindu temples and the Ganges River. He worked extremely hard to uplift his family.

B. Paternal Grandfather: Gokal Dhudshia (1864–1918)

On my father's side, my grandfather, Gokal, was the youngest son of my great-grandfather, Devasi. Grandfather Gokal was a hardworking, lower-middle-class farmer. He lived a basic, simple, and honest life. He never went to school. When he was twenty-two years old, the town of Shapur was established, and he was forced to move from Vanthali to Shapur. He worked extremely hard to build houses and establish farms and families in Shapur. He acquired more land. He was a devotee of the Vaishnava sect of Hinduism. He was excellent at singing *bhajan-kirtan* (devotional songs) and playing *tablas* (drums). He died before my birth, during the massive outbreak of plague in Gujarat. Since he died at an early age, in his fifties, my grandmother Kanku and my father took care of the big family of six brothers and two sisters.

C. Paternal Grandmother: Kanku Dhudshia (1864–1959)

I have particularly fond memories of my grandmother, Kanku, on my father's side. When I was growing up in a big, joint family, she was the head of the family. She was an extremely hardworking and strict lady; nothing could move without her permission. She controlled the joint family for many years. The joint family worked in harmony and prospered a lot under her and my father's leadership. They acquired more land and built houses. When she got old, she gave up control of the joint family living, and she let her four sons live individually. The farm operations were run by a joint family. She liked her eldest son and lived with him after the family division. After a few years, she distributed the joint farm property to her sons. When her eldest son died, she lived with her youngest and most prosperous son, Jasmat, in Vanthali. She developed a benign tumor under her left ear. The tumor kept growing, but she never allowed anyone to remove it. She died at the age of ninety-four, due to complications from the tumor.

D. Maternal Grandfather: Bhagavan Kanjia (1883–1952)

My grandfather, Bhagavan (which means "god"), on my mother's side, was a quite simple, poor farmer. He lived a basic, simple life in a small village called Dhandhusar, a farming and dairy town, only five kilometers from my birth town of Shapur. He was uneducated. With hard work on a small piece of land, he raised four boys and five girls. During his time, education was unheard of in small villages. None of his children got any education. They all remained in poverty for one more generation. He never had any luxury. Grandfather Bhagavan was a very honest, hardworking, soft-spoken, and loving person. No one ever took his picture. He used to wear white *chorano* (narrow trousers) with a short, pleated shirt, and a turban. He used to visit Shapur often, on his horse, for shopping. I loved his horse. While visiting Shapur, he always put me in charge of taking care of his horse. Whenever he visited us, he used to bring sweets and fruits for us. We all looked forward to his visits. He died in his seventies, due to a stroke.

E. Maternal Grandmother: Moti Kanjia (1885–1990)

Figure 1.3: Grandmother Moti.

Like my grandfather, Bhagavan, on my mother's side, my grandmother Moti (which means "pearl") was a quite simple woman without any education. She helped my grandfather to raise their nine children. She lived a basic, simple life with Grandfather Bhagavan. She was a very hardworking, honest, calm, and loving person. I have lots of fond memories of her kind and caring nature.

Whenever I visited her in Dhandhusar, she treated me with love, hugs, and goodies. I will never forget her for giving me big servings of yogurt, butter, and ghee on my chapatis (flatbread). She never traveled outside a fifty-mile radius of her birthplace. Since she lived a basic life, she was a content, satisfied, and happy person most of the time. She did not know anything about the changing world and politics. She never bothered anyone for her personal needs. She lived for more than one hundred years (the exact age was unknown when she died). She died in 1990 of old-age complications. Fortunately, both of my kids, Neha and Neel, had an opportunity to meet her.

Figure 1.4: Father, Hansraj.

1.3 VISIONARY AND INSPIRING PARENTS

A. Father: Hansraj Dhudshia (1904–1999)

My father, Hansraj (which means "king of swans"), was a very hardworking, honest, and forward-thinking man of vision. He loved education. He never had an opportunity to receive an education for himself. He gave up school after fourth grade. However, he had a deep appreciation and love for education. He made sure that his younger brothers and his children were given adequate opportunities for education. Only his youngest brother, Jasmat, and I took advantage of his keen desire.

My father was born and raised in Shapur. He had five brothers and two sisters. At that time, Shapur was a small town with limited amenities. It had only one elementary school that taught up to fourth grade. Very few people used to go to a bigger town for further education. My father had to quit education after fourth grade and started helping his father in farming.

After my grandfather died at an early age, my father and my grandmother took responsibility for the large, joint family of thirty-five members. My father was only fourteen years old then. My grandmother Kanku and he kept the joint family working together and prospering. After his father's death, the Dhudshia family bought more land and residential property. My father mostly worked on farms and managed the financials of the joint family. He was a family contact person for selling farm products and buying family needs. However, he had a deep desire to get out of farming. He and his younger brother Ladha ran a small grocery store for five years in Shapur. After it got burned, they never reopened it. He started working on farms again.

He could not convince either of my elder brothers to get a more formal education. He insisted that I must get more education. He assured me that he would do anything, in his power and within his ability, to support my education. Because of his persistence and support, I was able to go to Junagadh (seven miles away from Shapur) for my middle school and high school education. He was supportive of my college education and my coming to America. He was ready to sell his land to send me to America for higher education. He was a prime motivator for my getting MSME (master of science in mechanical engineering), and PhD degrees.

He never traveled much until I came to America. He did a pilgrimage to India with the money I sent from my first paycheck. He was very thrilled by my well-deserving gesture. He also visited Mumbai (Bombay) when Manju was coming to America.

After my mother died in 1968, he started easing off of the farm work and started helping around the house, such as getting vegetables, *datans* (toothbrushes made from tree branches), grocery supplies, etc. Later, his knee joints degenerated, and he became almost immobile. For the last twenty years of his life, he spent his time in his room, performing puja (praying), reading books and newspapers, receiving visitors, talking, and eating.

My elder brother Devraj and I came up with an agreement to take good care of our father in his old age. I supplied the necessary monetary and moral support, and my brother Devraj and his wife, Mithibhabhi (with help from Shambhai, his wife, Savita, and their children) provided daily necessities. Since my brother Devraj was a devoted son, he took good care of our father.

Since he had a keen desire to visit America, his passport was prepared, and a visitor's visa (using my sponsorship) was obtained. However, he didn't know English. We were looking for a responsible travel companion. We could not find any for a while. Before his visa expired, Manju and I made a special trip to India to bring him to America with us. At the last minute, he changed his mind and decided not to visit America. We were heartbroken and felt bad about not being able to satisfy his keen desire.

My father was a staunch devotee of the Vaishnava sect of Hinduism. However, he was not a blind follower of the sect. He modified some of his views of Vaishnavism after one of our relatives introduced him to the Swaminarayan sect's views.

He wore a big, white turban with a shirt, coat, and chorano (narrow trousers), all made from white cotton cloth. Whenever we visited him, Neel loved my father's turban.

My father never had any major diseases like diabetes, high blood pressure, cancer, ulcers, or glaucoma. The only problem he had was his knees, which got worse with his age. He passed on to us good genes.

When he died, he was almost ninety-six years old. He died on March 19, 1999, of old-age complications, without any major disease.

I am so happy that my father had an opportunity to enjoy the "fruits of his vision", improved family living standards, and relish the luxury of life during his later life. My mother did not.

Neha and Neel both had opportunities to meet him several times.

B. Mother: Ganga Dhudshia/Ganga Kanjia (1905–1968)

Figure 1.5: Mother, Ganga.

My mother, Ganga, was born and raised in a small farming and dairy town called Dhandhusar (five kilometers north of Shapur), in a loving and caring Kanjia family. She lived basic, simple childhood life. She had four brothers and four sisters. She was the second eldest sister. She was married to my father at an early age of four years (child marriage).

Her first name, Ganga, came from the biggest and most sacred river of India, the Ganga (Ganges) River. Just like the Ganga River, she cared for her family selflessly and with a big heart.

She never went to school. She was illiterate, but she had lots of common sense. When she was a young wife, she was a member of a big, joint Dhudshia family. Her day used to start at 4:00 a.m. when she would prepare food, grind wheat and bajra (millet) flour, churn curd to make butter, milk the buffalo, clean the buffalo and cow barns, and feed the kids. After her morning chores, she worked on the family farms during the day and took care of her children at night. After our joint family got divided, she kept herself busy with farm work and buffalo raising. She ran her own small dairy business that generated supplemental income for our family.

My mother's family prospered more than that of any one of her siblings because she married an educated husband and raised educated children.

She never had the luxury of anything. She owned very few pieces of good clothing (saris) and jewelry. She didn't travel more than one hundred miles from her birthplace until she was in her late fifties (after I came to America). The first time she went more than one hundred miles away was when she went on a pilgrimage with my father in 1964. Later, she traveled to Mumbai when Manju was coming to America (in September 1965).

My mother was an extremely hardworking, simpleminded, honest, and loving mother, and she was a devoted wife. When I was in elementary school, she used to take me with her to the Somnath temple and the Satadhar temple, her very favorite religious places. She never understood anything about school and college. But she always supported me in going to school and college. She always wanted me to be an engineer. In her simple mind, an engineer meant the person who operated a railway engine. When I was in engineering college, she always came to the railway station, carrying my bags on her head and saying goodbye with tears (of joy) in her eyes.

My last memory of her is etched in my mind forever. On the day of my first departure for America from my village of Shapur, on August 15, 1963, she came to the railway station to bid goodbye to me, along with many other family members, relatives, and friends. After I found my seat on the train, she came near the window, gave me her blessings, and said, "Goodbye, son, and come back soon after your education." On her face, I saw joy and pride in her son going to America, and the pain of letting her son go so far away. I could never forget her face which showed her mixed feelings. On that day, I did not know that it was the last time I would see her face. Unfortunately, she never had a chance to see me again, and her family prospered after I came to America. She died on January 31, 1968, due to a brain hemorrhage for an unknown reason. We visited India in April 1968. One of her wishes to play grandma with my daughter, Neha, never materialized.

2

EMERGING CHILD

2.1 Primitive Childhood

I was born in a small town called Shapur (as described in detail in the following section A), on December 2, 1939. My actual birthday never got recorded anywhere. The date is based on a ration card registration, and on my mother's recollection of my birthday on the Hindu calendar. Later, my official birthday became July 1, 1939, when my father first enrolled me in elementary school on July 1, 1946, and the principal deducted seven years from the enrollment date.

When I was a child, I was a member of a large, joint family of more than thirty family members who lived together. My grandfather Gokal died at an early age, leaving the entire family's responsibility to my father and my grandmother Kanku. Being in a large, joint family, there was little individual attention given to any child, including me, in the family.

When I was around six years old, our joint family was divided into four families. At that time, my parent's family had seven members: my parents, three boys, and two girls.

Our house consisted of only one multipurpose room, a covered front porch, and a kitchen. Its walls were constructed of local quarry stones with rough surfaces and irregular sizes. The roof had locally made clay singles. The floor was laced with a mixture of cow dung and clay. The house had a barn and a farm equipment shed in the backyard. We also used the backyard as an open-air toilet facility. During the nighttime, the front courtyard was used to tie down buffaloes and cows on the perimeter. It had no running water, no electricity, no furniture, and no bathroom. The kitchen had two simple wood-burning stoves. At dark, we used kerosene lamps for light inside and kerosene lanterns as a moving light source. For sleeping, we used cots made of raw wood frames and coconut fiber strings. For mattresses, we used homemade quilts made from old clothes and cotton. We called them *godada*. I always slept in the front courtyard (except when it rained), surrounded by buffaloes and cows.

I had no toys to play with. I played around the house in dirt and barns. My maternal uncle (Mama) gave us a toy bullock cart to share among our three brothers. I never got to play with it. One of my favorite toys was a scrap piece of railway track connector, which I would hang to make a bell and ring as a make-believe railway station bell. My other favorite hobby was playing with dirt and preparing make-believe farms with irrigation systems. I loved to go to farms and hang around elders working on a farm and eating fresh farm products.

My mother used to work on the farms during the day. At night, she used to take care of her children, including me (I was one of her five children), and the buffaloes and cows.

My childhood meals were quite simple, basic, and the same almost every day. I ate yogurt and bajra (millet) *rotla* (thick flatbread) in the morning; bajra rotla and dal (beans) or vegetables at lunch; and *khichadi* (cooked rice and bean), milk, and bajra rotla for dinner. For snacks, I ate homegrown peanuts and *gol* (jaggery). When I was young, wheat roti (a thin flatbread) was a luxury, and our family could not afford it at that time.

My mother cooked meals on a simple stove that burned wood, hay, and cow dung chips. I ate in a simple German silver bowl and sat on the floor. There were no spoons or forks. I ate with my hands.

During my childhood, I wore pajamas (with drawstrings), shirts, and caps, all custom-made from the same rough, white cotton cloth material. I had

only two sets of pajamas, shirt, and cap—one I wore and the other would be waiting to be washed. My mother used to wash them every three to four weeks. I didn't have shoes until I started middle school. Unfortunately, I do not have a single photograph from my childhood. My first photo was taken when I was in tenth grade (Figure 2.2).

A. My Birth Town: Shapur

My birth town, Shapur, is currently in the Junagadh district (kingdom) in Gujarat, India.

Figure 2.1: Typical childhood dress.

It has existed since ancient times. The name means "habitat for snakes" because it was infested with snakes and had many snakebite-related deaths. It was neither well laid out nor a protected town.

In the late 1880s, the king (Navab) of the Junagadh kingdom decided to combine three small farming villages into one bigger village around the Shapur territory. The expansion was well planned with: (i) straight roads and square blocks, (ii) a fortress that was thirty feet high and four feet wide around the town, (iii) a king's palace in the center of the town and a playground in front of the king's palace, and (iv) an elementary school for boys and girls. The fortress had four gates, one in each direction. It gave protection against wild animals and invaders. Once the gates were closed, no one could come in or go out without going through the security check. The location of the town was ideal for the water supply. It had a river on the south side and a small creek on the north side. Both had continuous freshwater flow year-round.

Once the planned roads and fortress were built, the king forced the two nearby small villages into Shapur from 1882 to 1886. The king also forced one family member of each farming family living in the town of Vanthali to move to Shapur. Every family who moved to Shapur was given a free residential plot to build houses and stores.

My grandfather Gokal was one of the Dhudshia family members who was forced to move to Shapur.

By the time I was born, Shapur had a population of over three thousand. It had a railway station, three oil mills, a cotton packing factory, a rock sugar factory, a postal and telegraph office, a new summer palace with a garden outside the fortress, one mosque on Main Street and one outside the town, a few Hindu temples around the town, and two elementary schools (one for boys and another for girls).

B. Political Environment during my Childhood

When I was a child, Shapur was a part of the Junagadh kingdom, which was ruled by a Muslim king (Navab). The majority of the population were Hindus; however, since the king was a Muslim, we had to follow the Islamic rules and customs, such as that weekends consisted of Thursdays and Fridays.

The king may have been ignorant, but his cronies were taking advantage of the Hindu population, in the name of the king. They would take from any Hindu family anything they liked, and they would order Hindu families to do anything for them for free. This was like slavery. No one could say or do anything about it. If you complained, they would punish you and/ or kill you. The worst thing they were doing was taking away beautiful young Hindu ladies and raping them.

See chapter 14.1 for a memorable event that happened during this time.

Most of the teachers were Muslim, and they were ruthless. They were giving preference to Muslim students. If you were not Muslim, growing up was very rough.

When India became independent in 1947, British rulers created two countries: India and Pakistan. And they gave the choice to the local king to align either with India or with Pakistan. The king of the Junagadh kingdom aligned with Pakistan, despite the Hindu majority. This was a very weird situation. A part of Pakistan was within India, like Dallas

County is a part of Mexico. Once the kingdom aligned with Pakistan, his cronies terrorized the kingdom. Looting, raping, unpaid forced labor, obeying Muslims, and living under constant fear became widespread. This harsh situation became unbearable, and it forced some of us (me and my siblings) to migrate to the nearby Hindu kingdom. In November 1948, the Indian Army and the local Hindu militias, under the leadership of Sardar Vallabhbhai Patel, attacked the king and forced him to leave the kingdom. Once the king left with his cronies, the Junagadh kingdom had the plebiscite to join India. After this change in government, the political environment changed. The Junagadh kingdom became an integral part of India's state of Gujarat. Those who migrated came back, including us. I restarted my second-grade education in Shapur.

2.2 ELEMENTARY SCHOOL EDUCATION

I started at the boys' elementary school in Shapur on July 1, 1946. At that time, my town was under a Muslim ruler. Most of the teachers were Muslim. They were extremely strict and ruthless in disciplining the children. Beating and other physical punishments were quite common. Most of the elementary school education was reading and writing, memorizing elementary arithmetic, geography, and some science.

As described in the previous section, when I was in second grade, India gained independence (August 15, 1947), and our Muslim king (Navab) decided to align with Pakistan. My father sent all his children to my sister's place, in another kingdom under a Hindu king, just twenty-five miles away in Pipalia. (See chapter 14.2 for details.) I continued my elementary education in Pipalia in second grade without any learning. When the kingdom reinstated alignment with India, I came back to Shapur, and I restarted in the second grade. I lost one year of education in the temporary migration. Since Navab left for Pakistan, his palace in the center of Shapur was converted into a boys' elementary school. The education system was changed to align with Gandhi's philosophy called Sarvodaya. In that system, all the students were treated with respect, care, and love. Nationalistic and patriotic feelings were extremely high. Teachers were called bhais (brothers). All the students were required to spin cotton to make cloth and clean their own classrooms and school facilities. Study books were changed. The weekend off-days were changed from Thursdays and Fridays to Saturdays and Sundays. The national language (Hindi) was introduced in the fifth grade.

I quit school for a month, between the fourth and fifth grades. (See details in Chapter 13.1.)

During my fifth- and sixth-grade education, I was exposed to Gandhi's philosophy, with lots of nationalistic feelings. I almost joined a new schooling system based on serving and uplifting the community without English influence. My father did not like that style, because they did not have the English language in the school curriculum. He knew that to become an engineer or a doctor, one needed to learn the English language. At that time, English was (and still is) very widely used in India. He insisted that I should go to another middle school with the English language in the curriculum.

During my elementary school education, I was an exceptionally good student, and I was always at the top of my class. Since I was an obedient and smart student, all the teachers liked me.

2.3 MIDDLE SCHOOL EDUCATION (JUNE 1953–JUNE 1956)

There was no middle school in Shapur. They had a seventh-grade class, but without the English language in the curriculum. My father wanted me to go to a school where they had English in the curriculum. I had to go either to Vanthali (three miles away) or Junagadh (seven miles away). I started seventh grade in Vanthali. I did not like the school because it was a madrassa-style school with Muslim students in the majority. My father took me to Junagadh, a nearby big city within commuting distance by train, and tried to enroll me in the City Middle School, Junagadh (Shree Narsinh Vidyamandir), near the railway station. I was denied admission because the school in Shapur had a seventh-grade class. However, on my father's insistence to include English in my curriculum, he made a special petition, in person, to the district's school superintendent. (See Chapter 14.3 for details.) Our petition was approved and I (along with other four students from Shapur) was admitted to the City Middle School, Junagadh, in seventh grade, in June 1953. I took the train from Shapur to go to school and came back. It was a twenty-minute train ride, one way, every day. We were five students going together every day.

The school was noticeably bigger compared to the Shapur school. There were eight classes just for seventh grade. I started learning two new subjects—English language and elementary calculus—from this grade.

Studying in Junagadh was a new, life-changing experience for me. I—being from a small-town, ordinary farmer's family—looked very backward (village boy) in culture, language, and dress. (I used to wear pajamas, a shirt, and a Gandhi topi hat.) However, I was smart in studying. I started making good grades and capturing top ranks in the class during my first semester there. Because of this, many city boys ignored my village look, and we became exceptionally good friends, and they helped me to polish my outlook. Students from Kadwa Patel Boarding, who were in the school for two or three years before me, also helped me to change my outlook. I gave up my Gandhi topi hat, pajamas, and clay slate and adopted a new look with no hat, combed hair, English pants, and a notebook, instead of clay slate, for class notes. I learned a lot from this exposure to city boys. My parents were supportive of the changes and the associated expenses. They were committed to my education at any cost.

My seventh-grade classroom teacher was Shivlal Vyas, a truly kind, mild-mannered, old-fashioned teacher who liked my attitude, behavior, and good grades. I became one of his favorite students.

The transition from seventh grade to eighth grade was a little rough. By mistake, school officials put me in a class with Muslim students learning Urdu as a classical language. I was supposed to be in the class with the Hindu students learning Sanskrit (the mother language of many Indian languages). I was very miserable for a while. I had no guts to go to the principal and request a change of class. I thought about quitting school. Meanwhile, my seventh-grade teacher (Shivlal Vyas) ran into me and inquired why I was not in his eighth-grade class. He understood the mistake and immediately transferred me to his class (with the Sanskrit language). I became a happy camper again and continued my forward march. I completed eighth grade in the city's middle school with first class.

I remained in the city's middle school for the ninth grade, too. I completed the grade with a first-class grade. My classroom teacher, Mr. I. L. Vyas, gave me a prize (Rs. 2 cash) for being first in the class.

On a typical school day in middle school, I used to get up around 6:00 a.m. and help my mother around the house and outside the buffalo barn. I ate a breakfast of yogurt and bajra rotla (thick millet flatbread). I did homework and reading, then I ate a little snack and went to the railway station to catch the 10:00 a.m. train to Junagadh. My class started at 11:00 a.m. The lunch break was from 2–3 p.m. Most of the time, I did not bring any food from home for lunch. I used to buy two bananas (for one anna) for my lunch. Sometimes, I had to run errands at lunchtime to buy a few things, which were not available in Shapur, from the Junagadh market for our family. My classes ended at 5:00 p.m. The return train, to Shapur, left at 5:10 p.m. I had to run from class to catch the train. Once I came back home, I ate some snacks, helped around the house, and did some homework. Our family dinner used to be between 7:00 and 8:00 p.m. At dinner, we ate *khichdi*, bajra rotla, fresh milk, pickles, and sometimes leftover veggies from lunch. After dinner, I hung around the family and did some homework and reading. I used to go to sleep around 9:00 or 10:00 p.m.

During the middle-school summer vacations, I used to help on farms with irrigating crops, harvesting mangos, and laying fertilizer. Sometimes, I took our buffaloes for grazing. When I was in middle school, a few neighborhood friends and I formed volleyball and cricket teams in Shapur with support from *Gram Panchayat* (the town government) and local businesses. I played both sports during the summer but never became an expert in either sport.

2.4 HIGH SCHOOL EDUCATION (JUNE 1956–JUNE 1958)

I joined Junagadh High School (Swami Vivekanand High School) for the tenth and eleventh grades. Now I was used to the city environment and large student body. This transition was quite easy. During both years, I stayed with my parents and commuted to high school from Shapur. I started a study group with six other Shapur students where we got together after dinner, stayed overnight in a room provided by the *Gram Panchayat* (town government), and studied in the evenings and early mornings, starting at 4:00 a.m. Since I had limited space to study in my parents' house, this study room was beneficial to me. This helped me to get very good grades and broaden my horizon. I tried to learn typing for a few months (without any success) when I was in tenth grade.

During the Diwali vacation in 1956, I went on a tour of Bombay (Mumbai) with my friends from Shapur. This was my first exposure to a big international city with crowded local trains and buses, huge markets and showrooms, flashing electrical signs, an airport, museums, and big factories. I also visited my cousin-sister Labhuben (who was the matchmaker for me and Manju) and her relatives living in the neighborhoods. I and other friends were so eager to see the airplanes taking off, and we went into a restricted area close to the runway. We were detained and released after questioning. I am sure we must have looked like fools from a small village.

When I entered the eleventh grade, Junagadh High School ran out of space, and it changed to a two-shift operation. The new timing did not synchronize with the train schedule. I was forced to use other transportation. I tried the bus, but its schedule was unpredictable. I tried Patel Boarding House, but I did not like the environment. Finally, I bought a bicycle and commuted (approximately eight miles each way) to and from the high school by bicycle.

Figure 2.2: High school student, Vallabh, summer 1957.

Eleventh grade was the final year of the high school education. All students were required to take a secondary school certificate (SSC) exam (also known as a metric exam) at the end of the year. The final year of high school was especially important because the grades in the SSC were used for admission in the colleges. I passed the SSC exam with first class distinction (equivalent to an A+). I took seven subjects (Gujarati, Hindi, English, general science, physics and chemistry, arithmetic, and mathematics) in the SSC.

I was the second in the Dhudshia family to complete my high school education. My uncle Jasmat was the first in our family. However, I was the first one to go to college.

During my final year of high school, I got an opportunity to know and become friends with Mr. S. R. Velankar and his wife Suman. This acquaintance benefited me a lot, as detailed in chapter 9.5: Enriching Friends.

3

MATURING MAN

3.1 JUNIOR COLLEGE EDUCATION (JUNE 1958–APRIL 1960)

I was thrilled to start my college education. My family was proud of me because I was the first one from our family to go to college. They were excited about my going to college, even though no one knew about college education. They were supportive of my college education.

Figure 3.1: Bahauddin College, Junagadh.

I selected Bahauddin College in Junagadh for my junior college education. I was familiar with the city, and it was only seven miles from my hometown. It also had the lowest tuition fee. I selected the science group, which prepared students for either engineering or medical careers.

My first year of college started on June 20, 1958. My college education brought many big changes in my life. The first time I left my parents' home and lived in a college hostel (dormitory), I learned to live with and socialize with students from many different towns, races, cultures, economic levels, studying styles, and college years. The teaching style was different from what I had been used to in high school. We had almost fifty students—boys, and girls—in my science class. It included lectures for large groups and practical laboratories for small groups.

Figure 3.2: Collegian Vallabh, 1958.

This was the first time I had been exposed to coeducation with female students. The college education changed my dressing style. Most of the students were looking outstanding by dressing well and behaving smartly. I had to follow the trend. Since I was getting good grades, it was easy for me to get recognized on campus.

This was my first experience working closely with a female student. My lab desk partner was a female student. We shared lab equipment and helped each other in the experiments. I established a conversational relationship with her.

During my first year, I joined the National Cadet Corps (NCC), an extracurricular activity, similar to ROTC. It exposed me to the military world. I enjoyed learning the military discipline exercises, knowing different rifles and guns, shooting, and camping. This program showed me an appreciation for the work of the military personnel defending India.

I learned to study with a big group of students living in the hostel. There was always someone to chitchat with me and kill time. I was a very disciplined and goal-oriented student. I balanced my time between studying and enjoying college life. As a result, I completed my first year of college at the top of my class and received a merit scholarship.

Once I started living in the hostel, I had to get used to non-home-cooked food. The quality of the hostel mess food was poor. The mess operator was looking for profit rather than the quality of the food. Many students were in the same boat that I was in. We all got together and complained to the hostel rector, who advised us to start a cooperative self-managed mess. Which we did. The hostel provided the facility for cooking and dining. We hired a cook, appointed a manager from our group, and shared expenses equally. We got the best quality ingredients and managed the menu. This worked out well. There were no more complaints about the hostel food.

Before the start of the second year, I had to decide about my future career: engineering or medicine. My parents had neither any clue nor any preference. I would have succeeded in either one. However, I loved mathematics more than biology, so I decided to take Group A (with mathematics) which was required for admission to engineering college. My second year of college was critical to getting admission to the engineering college. Since I was a scholar in my first year of college, all my friends respected me, and they always wanted my advice to prepare for the exam. The college faculty was also kind to me and helped me to maintain my good grades. I studied hard and completed the second year with first-class honors and was on top of the class. This made getting admission to the engineering college quite easy.

During the vacation, I prepared for the entrance exam for admission to IIT (Indian Institute of Technology), the top engineering college in India. I had to go to Mumbai (Bombay) to take the entrance exam. I did not do well in the exam because it was in English. I was not yet used to the English medium of instruction.

Mohan (my first cousin) and Magan (my second nephew) came with me to Mumbai. After my exam, we took a tour of south India and visited Pune, Sangli, Kolhapur, Satara, Koyna, etc., and met many of our caring and welcoming relatives who had settled in that region. During this trip, the most interesting place I visited was the Koyna hydroelectric power complex, an engineering marvel. I was flabbergasted by the size of the lake, dam, and tunnels, and the powerhouse with huge turbines and generators just like the Hoover Dam in America. Since I was going to start engineering college soon, this visit gave me a preview of my engineering career.

3.2 ENGINEERING COLLEGE EDUCATION (JUNE 1960–APRIL 1963)

Since my childhood, I have had an aptitude for engineering. I used to play with a power/motion system using empty thread pools and homemade rope belts, making them turn and using discarded power cells (batteries) to make an electrical grid in the home with small light bulbs. We had oil engines on the farms to pump water. Whenever I went to the farms, I used to watch the engine turning and pumping water for hours. At that time, I did not know that my dream of becoming an engineer was going to be realized. The start of engineering college was the beginning of realizing my childhood dream.

Figure 3.3: Lukhdhirji Engineering College.

I got admission easily in the Lukhdhirji Engineering College in Morbi, Gujarat. I selected the mechanical engineering group.

The college building was originally a gorgeous palace of King Lukhdhirji on the bank of the Machhu River. It was converted into the engineering college and was named after him.

Engineering college broadened my horizon much more. Now, I was among the best of the best students from all over the Saurashtra region (a region of Gujarat). We also had a few students from all over India. It was an all-male student body.

I had to learn different learning styles, which included theory and practical engineering assignments. This was the first time the medium of instruction and textbooks were in English. I had to start dealing with new faculty and earn their respect. All the courses—such as heat engines, engineering mechanics, theory of dynamics, engineering drawing, mechanical workshop, structural mechanics, metallurgy, etc.—were new to me. The curriculum also included lots of practical assignments in drawing, workshops, heat engines, and surveys. Since I enjoyed all the courses, I did not have to work hard to get good grades. I had a goal to become an engineer. I kept the goal in front of all other activities. I managed to balance social and academic activities and fully enjoyed all of them.

At the end of the first year, I got recognition as a scholar and became a favorite and exemplary student in the eyes of most of the faculty. My engineering drawings were framed and put on the classroom walls as examples of good work. This made my campus life very satisfying. I completed the first year with the first class and was on top of the class.

During the first year, I received scholarships from the Government of India, the Science and Research Cultural Ministry, and the Patel Mohanlal Gokaldas Scholarship Fund. These scholarships were enough for my financial needs. My parents were relieved of my financial burden.

During my first year of engineering college, I made many new friends from all over India. Among them were Mahesh Dixit (who later immigrated to America with my help), Bhagvanji Raiyani (who became a well-known builder and settled in Mumbai), Kirit K. Shah (who also settled in Mumbai and worked in his father's business), and Jaysukh Ranparia (who also immigrated to America with my help and sponsorship).

After a long first year of engineering college, the summer vacation was short. I visited our relatives and friends in the nearby area and helped my brother Devraj on the farms.

For my second year of engineering college, I chose the mechanical engineering group. This year was combined for mechanical and electrical engineering students. During the first semester, I participated in making an engineering model for a dam with automatic gates. Our model received the first prize. During the second semester of this year, my friend Jaysukh Ranparia and I took a challenge to manage the student co-op mess (eating facility). Greedy, dishonest student managers ran it very poorly. The food bills were high, and the food quality was poor. We turned the situation around with honesty, hard work, and vision. We provided excellent food with more variety and at a lower cost. Not only that, but we were also able to install ceiling fans in the dining room and provided uniforms for the serving staff.

I made many more friends and became a favorite student of many faculty members. I worked extremely hard and methodologically. I continued to be recognized as a scholar on campus. I continued enjoying college life by balancing studying and my social life. I completed my second year of engineering college with a first-class grade.

During the second year, I gave serious thought to going to America for further study, as detailed in the next chapter.

During the second year, I continued receiving scholarships from the Government of India, the Science and Research Cultural Ministry, and the Patel Mohanlal Gokaldas Scholarship Fund. These scholarships were enough for my financial needs. My parents were relieved of my financial burden again. Because I managed the lodging co-op mess, I had more cash than I needed for my educational expenses. I used the surplus cash to upgrade the kitchen in our house in Shapur and to install electrical wiring. During the 1962 summer vacation, I used my electrical engineering knowledge (my first real-life use of my engineering knowledge) to install electrical wiring in my house in Shapur.

Figure 3.4: Future engineer, spring, 1963.

My third and final year of engineering college was an important year of my career. I had two goals to achieve that year: keep up with my first-class grades and get admission to a reputable American university.

That year, I added one more dimension to my career by getting elected as a class representative (CR) of the Bachelor of Engineering-Mechanical (BE Mech) class in the student council. This was my first experience in representing a group of people. This gave me broad exposure and networking opportunities outside the academic world. I initiated many popular changes on the campus (within the power of the student council). I became an extremely popular CR. This position gave me many opportunities to represent my college and my class at many different occasions, and I got exposure to dignitaries.

That year, I took on more responsibility for my class. I organized a technical tour of North India during the Diwali vacation. This tour was a requirement to graduate, and it was funded by my engineering college. With help from a staff member (Associate Professor Gayatri Bhatt) and Mr. Khandhar, we developed an itinerary, made railway and boarding reservations, got permission to visit industrial plants, and blended the itinerary with sightseeing visits to tourist attractions. We visited industrial plants that were well-known in the mechanical engineering field, such as the Chittaranjan Locomotive Works (a railway engine manufacturing plant), Tata Motors plant, Bhilai steel manufacturing factory, National Physical Laboratory, National Instruments plant, coal mines, an air conditioner manufacturing plant, a structural steel manufacturing plant, etc. This tour showed me the use of engineering knowledge in real life, and it portrayed a picture of my future life. This tour also gave me an opportunity to visit well-known tourist attractions in North India, like the Hawa Mahal in Jaipur; Red Fort, the parliament house, Qutub Mīnār, and the Gandhi memorial in New Delhi; the Taj Mahal in Agra; the Ajanta Caves; Victoria Park in Kolkata (Calcutta); and Mumbai tourist attractions.

During the third year, I continued receiving scholarships from the Government of India, the Science and Research Cultural Ministry, and the Patel Mohanlal Gokaldas Scholarship Fund. These scholarships were enough for my financial needs. My parents were relieved of my financial burden again. I also managed the lodging co-op mess during the first semester. This allowed me to save funds for my preparation to go to America.

Figure 3.5: Mechanical engineering class of 1963.

My third year of engineering college was the most important and busiest year of my college career. I continued to be recognized as a scholar and a popular CR on campus. I continued enjoying college life, balancing studying and my social life. The end of my third year of engineering college was the end of my college life in India. I completed my final year with a first-class grade.

4

PRE-TRANSPLANTATION ACTIVITIES

4.1 Initial Thoughts about Transplantation into America

I did not know anything about America during my childhood. Not only that, but I also had never heard much about the country of America during middle school and high school. When I was in my first year of college, I met our neighbor's relative who was going to America, after graduating from engineering college, for further study. I took a keen interest in his adventure and learned a little bit about going to America for further study. This meeting gave me something to think about if I wanted to become an engineer.

When I started engineering college, my two professors had advanced degrees from American universities. I learned quite a bit from them about studying in America. When I was in the second year of my engineering studies, I started learning more about going to America for an advanced degree. Since I had a very good relationship with both my professors, they guided me and encouraged me to go to America for further study. At that time, there were limited advanced degree programs for engineering graduates in India. Before the end of my second year of engineering study, I decided to go to America after completing a bachelor's degree in engineering in India. During the summer vacation in 1962, I told my parents, my brother Devraj, and my uncle Jasmat about my plans to go to

America. Everyone was thrilled with my plans and supported my decision. They also assured me that they would do anything, within their ability, to make my plans materialize. With their assurance and blessings, I started activities to go to America for further study.

4.2 PLANNING FOR TRANSPLANTATION INTO AMERICA

During the first semester of my third and final year of engineering college, I had a goal to gain admission to a reputable American university. While working on the regular coursework, I started correspondence with American universities for admission information and applications. At the same time, I started collecting all the documents—such as certificates, grade transcripts, recognitions, awards, scholarships, recommendation letters, etc.—needed for admission to American universities. I got lots of help from mechanical engineering professors in selecting universities and preparing applications for admission to American universities.

I started getting admission to American universities right after the Christmas break of 1962. I got admission to the Illinois Institute of Technology, Purdue University, and Stanford University. With the help of Professor P. K. Patel, I decided to accept admission to the Illinois Institute of Technology (IIT), in Chicago, Illinois. My high school friend Vallabh Patel (Bhut) also got and accepted admission to the IIT. This was a relief to me because I knew that a familiar person would be with me in an unknown land.

After the end of the third year, and while waiting for the final exam results, I started preparing to go to America. The top priority was to collect the needed funds for my trip to America and for my educational expenses there. My parents did not have any spare funds for my education in America. They were ready to sell our land to raise the funds. I told them not to do that. Instead, we sought funds from our relatives. My uncle Jasmat and my uncle Vasharam came forward to lend me five thousand rupees. Soon after that, Govind Patel (our distant relative from Vanthali) gave two thousand rupees; my brother Devraj's father-in-law, Bhimaji Patel, gave one thousand rupees; my brother Vithal's father-in-law, Lakhman Patel, gave three thousand rupees; and my cousin-sister Jayaben's father-in-law, Chatrabhuj Patel, gave one thousand rupees. All the lenders of the funds were happy to lend me money for a noble cause, without any interest, binding papers, or assurance to repay. I could never forget their trust and support. I was lucky to have such generous, supportive, and selfless relatives.

While collecting funds, I was also preparing my passport and booking tickets to travel to America.

While preparing for my trip to America, the US Embassy and Consulates office in Mumbai invited all the Indian students, who had secured admission and a visa to go to America, for orientation to American campus life and society. They paid for all the travel, lodging, and boarding expenses. I attended the orientation. This gave me a preview of what would happen shortly. I did not understand why the US Embassy and Consulates had paid all the expenses for the orientation. Now, I think that was an incentive to attract bright international students to come to America.

4.3 Uprooting from the Land of Birth

Since this was my last summer vacation in India, I visited and spent quality time with each relative. After that summer, I never got such an opportunity again. Since I was the first from my town and relatives to go to America, everybody respected me for my achievements and the opportunity to go to America. My relatives and friends held many receptions about my going to America. I became close to Uncle Jasmat and his family and became his favorite nephew. I made him a proud uncle. He took a keen interest in my going to America and spent time with me to advise me and help me prepare.

I was preoccupied with the preparation for my trip to America, as detailed in chapter 6.3, and I had no time to think about marriage. I decided to continue preparations without getting married.

A. Leaving Hometown and Home

By the beginning of August 1963, I completed all the necessary formalities and preparations for my trip to America. My friend Vallabh Patel and I decided to travel by ship from Mumbai to Genova, Italy, and by train to London, England, via Paris, France, and then fly to America. This itinerary was the most economical.

The last two weeks were very emotional for me and my family. I spent quality time with my mother, father, brothers, sisters, and local friends. Since I was the first one from my town, they were proud of my achievements and my going to America. My local friends arranged a grand going-away party to celebrate my going to America. I visited my elementary and secondary schools, high school, and junior college, and I cherished the good times I'd had at those institutions.

The entire Shapur community, and my relatives, congratulated my parents for raising a son like me. They took pride and joy in such an occasion. However, my parents had the pain of letting me go away across oceans, from where I could not come back to meet them often. This was the beginning of my painful separation from my parents, siblings, house, hometown, friends, and motherland country. Many times, I had thoughts about my failure in America and its devastating results. I had no clear answer: Why was I going to America? Why was I leaving my family and motherland and going to a foreign country? The only answer I had was that I wanted to get an advanced degree in mechanical engineering, make some money to repay my expenses, and come back to India to settle down. I was wrong.

This was also the beginning of changing my family's standard of living. I proved that an ordinary farmer's son can change the family's standard of living by getting proper education and going to America. This had been my father's dream.

On the morning of August 15, 1963, I participated in the Indian Independence Day ceremony in my hometown of Shapur by hoisting and saluting the Indian tricolor national flag. I was very emotional and was trembling during the ceremony. This was my last salute to the national flag as an Indian citizen. After the ceremony, when I came home, I saw almost everyone at home in tears. Many times, I could not stop them, either. While doing other things, I started noticing mixed feelings on my mother's face, sometimes sad and other times full of pride. I was just wondering what may have been going through her simple mind. She did not know anything about schools, colleges, America, etc. The only thing she knew was that her son was going to America. After lunch, I sat down, in private, with her, my father, and my brother for last-minute advice, hugs, and blessings. She could not say anything. At that time, I did not know that this would be my last emotional meeting with her.

A huge crowd of relatives and friends came to our home and walked with me to the railway station to bid goodbye and to wish me good luck. Many came with flowers, garlands, sweets, coconuts, and rock sugars. This was a very emotional farewell from my home, my parents, my siblings, my friends, and my hometown. When the train arrived, an emotional chill went through my body. I took the final blessings of my parents and some elders by touching their feet, then I got on the train and settled in my seat near the window. When the train's departure whistle went off, I stuck out my head from the train, and I saw the Shapur railway station platform filled with well-wishing relatives and friends shouting and waving goodbye and good luck to me.

Watching them disappear from my sight created a long-lasting memory of their love, respect, and well-wishes. I considered myself fortunate to have so many caring and loving relatives and friends.

As the train departed the Shapur railway station, I felt like I was being uprooted from the place where I had grown up.

Several close relatives and friends had a tough time saying goodbye, so they came with me on the train for the next five train stops and returned from there.

The first stop of the train was Junagadh, the town where I had attended middle school, high school, and junior college. The Junagadh railway station was full of my local friends from the town. They came, with flowers and garlands, to bid me farewell and wish me good luck. For me, this was an emotional goodbye to the town where I'd spent seven years of my life studying.

My friend Vallabh Patel and his family joined us on the train for our journey to Mumbai.

My brother Devraj and my uncle Jasmat traveled with me to Mumbai to bid me farewell. On the way to Mumbai, we all stopped in Ahmedabad for one day to meet with local friends. We also attended a reception, organized for us by the Saurashtra Patidar Society. I was impressed by the Patidar community spirit. Vallabh Patel and I did not know any leader of the community. However, they wanted to show their pride in the Patidar community students who were going to America for further study.

We spent two days in Mumbai for last-minute shopping and to bid goodbye to local relatives. Just like in Ahmedabad, we also attended another high-spirited reception given by the Mumbai Patidar Samaj. I also took time out to say goodbye to Manju (whom I had met earlier for matrimonial purposes) at Labhuben's place, as detailed in chapter 6.3.

B. Leaving India

I had been waiting and preparing for this day for a long time. Finally, it had arrived. Monday, August 19, 1963, is one of the most memorable days in my life. Early in the morning, we took off to go to Ballard Pier in Mumbai Harbor. The local Patidar community had arranged for our transportation to the harbor. We exchanged final farewell words, received blessings from my brother Devraj and my uncle Jasmat, and got our group pictures taken with all our relatives and friends who came to say goodbye and wish us the best of luck.

Figure 4.1: Final photograph before leaving India, August 19, 1963.

After an emotional goodbye with relatives and friends, we went through immigration, checked in with the ship's (the *Roma*) personnel, and put our luggage in the assigned cabin. Soon after that, we came back to the deck and waited there until the ship departed the port. All the relatives and friends were still there at the dock. We exchanged the final words and waved goodbye. As the ship's departing whistle went off, a chill went through my body. As the ship retracted the anchoring cords and pulled away from the dock, it felt like my umbilical cord had just been cut off. I was separated from my motherland, and I was on my own support system. I, and most of the new passengers, stayed on the deck until the ship sailed away from the harbor and the Mumbai skyline faded.

Once I could not see the Mumbai skyline from the ship, I realized that I had left India, my home, my parents, my brothers, my sisters, my relatives, and my friends. The distance between them and I was increasing every minute. I was on a no-return journey from which I could come back easily to visit them. I became very emotional and cried in my cabin. Good memories of my past times in India went through my mind, and I felt very miserable and sick (homesick and seasick). The pain of such an event is unique. It cannot be described. One must experience it to understand the intensity of the pain.

It felt like I was a young, growing tree that had been dug out from its original place, crated, and was being shipped to an unknown place. No one knew where it would go. What kind of land would it be transplanted in? How would it reestablish its roots? What would the weather and other environments be like in which it would grow and blossom?

This journey was the end of my permanent residency in my motherland of India, and it was the beginning of my transplantation into America.

4.4 ON THE WAY TO THE PROMISED LAND: AMERICA

My first night on the ship was horrible. I started remembering relatives and my home. I could not believe that I was not there anymore. The pain was so intense that I thought about returning home from London. That was neither possible nor practical. I had to continue my journey to the promised land of America.

My buddy from middle school and high school, Vallabh Patel, and his friend Pravin Sheladia were with me on the ship journey. We all stayed in the same cabin. We comforted and supported each other to overcome the pain of leaving India.

My seasickness continued for a day. The ship's doctor came by and gave me some medicine and advised me to eat as much as I could and to keep my stomach full. We went to the dining room, and I had my first lunch on the ship. Slowly, the seasickness started subsiding. However, homesickness was still lingering.

After a couple of days on the ship, I felt better, and I started enjoying the ship's amenities and atmosphere. There were more than two hundred Indian passengers, mostly students, on the ship; therefore, they employed Indian cooks to cater to the Indian passengers. The cooks used to consult us for the next day's menu. We started enjoying three meals a day, plus afternoon tea, and night snacks. This was my first experience eating anything other than typical Gujarati food and plenty of fruits, juices, ice creams, breads, cakes, cookies, jams, and jellies. This was my first exposure to Western people, and their culture and dress. We watched their dancing, drinking, and swimming parties. We had no guts to participate in any of those activities. However, there were others, like Indian movies, playing cards, chitchatting, and looking at the sea in the middle of nowhere. This journey also taught me some Western etiquette, like not going to the dining room in my pajamas, using public manners, giving courtesy to ladies first, saying thank you, etc. I also made many new friends during the journey.

The first stop of our ship's journey was at the Port of Suez in Egypt, located at the south end of the Suez Canal. Since the canal can handle only one-way traffic, our ship had to wait there for one day before entering the canal. Instead of waiting on the ship, a few old and new friends decided to explore the port town on foot. After being on the ship for eight days, walking on the ground felt delightful. This was the first time I put a step into a foreign land, Egypt. I had never been out of India. We took a walking tour of the town, tested local foods, visited the World War II memorial, experienced and witnessed Arab culture, and did window shopping.

On the following day, instead of going on the ship through the Suez Canal, some of us took a quick one-day bus trip to Cairo and joined the ship in the Port of Alexandria at the north end of the canal. I was very much impressed with the city of Cairo, its museums with golden statues, and their ornaments and beds. The sizes of the pyramids were amazing. This quick trip to Cairo became very memorable. I visited Cairo again in 1968 while going to India.

The ship also stopped at Naples and Milan in Italy. We had the opportunity at both places to take walking tours of the cities for a few hours. The last stop of our ship was Genova, Italy. We landed there and took a train to Paris, without doing any sightseeing. We had a seven-hour stop in Paris. We took advantage of our free time and took a taxi to the Eiffel Tower. We took a walking tour of the nearby area and visited the shopping center and park. We had no spare money to take the elevator to the top of the Eiffel Tower. I was impressed by the cleanliness of the city and shopping area. However, I didn't get a chance to experience French hospitality.

From Paris, we took trains and a short boat ride and arrived in London on September 3, 1963. We stayed at the foreign student council hostel. This was the first day of staying by ourselves. We did not know what to eat or where to go. Someone directed us to go to a nearby cafeteria. We ordered coffee, paid the bill, and came back and ordered a tomato omelet. I knew local people must have been laughing at us. The next day, we shipped our excess luggage by ship to the Illinois Institute of Technology (IIT) in Chicago, and we did some shopping. I bought an overcoat and a shirt. Harish Patel (Vallabh Patel's other friend) joined us for the rest of the journey to America. He was also going to attend IIT with us.

On the morning of September 5, we went to the airport in London and took a short Air France flight to Paris. This was my first experience flying in an airplane. It was not as frightening as I had expected. After a short stop in Paris, we took the Air France fight to New York, in the United States. This was my first exposure to a long (nine hours) plane flight, plane amenities, food, and confinement in my seat.

We (Vallabh Patel, Harish Patel, and I) arrived in New York at the John F. Kennedy International Airport, where we cleared immigration and took our first steps into the promised land of America. I became very emotional about taking my first step in America. I was very much impressed with the modern airport terminals and transport systems. We took the airport bus to the local TWA terminal and took a flight to Chicago. When we arrived in Chicago, we did not know where to go. We had never thought about it. We did not know anybody in Chicago. A fellow traveler took us to the travelers' aide's desk. The desk attendant called IIT, but no one answered due to the Labor Day holiday. He arranged for us to stay in Chicago's downtown YMCA. We took a bus to the YMCA and settled in the room. This was the end of my exciting journey from India to America. I learned a lot, but not enough, from this seventeen-day journey.

5

FRESHLY TRANSPLANTED IN THE PROMISED LAND: AMERICA

5.1 INITIAL SHOCK OF THE TRANSPLANTATION

We three (Vallabh Patel, Harish Patel, and I) did not know anything about living in America. The orientation that we had attended in Mumbai did not cover living outside of the campus. On our first day in America, there was no one to guide us. It looked like we arrived in Chicago's downtown from a jungle. Our dress, our language, and our manners looked very weird. We could not fully understand the language. We were not much familiar with American currency yet. We did not know where and how to shop for food (groceries) and other necessities. We did not know how to use local transportation. However, it took very little time to learn to live in America.

Some of our incidents of learning to live in America were funny, memorable, and full of hilarious occasions.

Once we settled in our YMCA room, we wanted to eat something. We had pickles in our bag, so we thought about going out and buying a loaf of bread. First, we went to the YMCA's cafeteria. We did not see bread; we had no guts to ask for any. We went outside of the YMCA. Most of the businesses were closed because of the Labor Day holiday. We took a walk on the street and found a cafeteria displaying bread. We went in and asked for twenty slices of bread. The cashier said they did not sell bread on its own. Then he realized that we were strangers in the town, so he gave us slices of bread and asked for thirty cents. Since we were not familiar with the currency, we showed him a handful of coins and asked him to take the appropriate amount. We had slices of bread, and now we wanted butter. One of us remembered seeing that the YMCA cafeteria had slices of butter. We went back to the YMCA cafeteria, picked up twenty slices of butter, put them on a tray, and stood in line to pay for them. Everyone in the line must have been giving us strange looks. When we came to the cashier, she said, "Sir, we do not sell butter slices; you get them free with the bread slices." We did not know what to do, so we left the butter slices on the tray and started walking away. But the cashier called us back and gave us the butter slices, free of charge. We went to our room and ate bread slices (untoasted) with butter and pickles. This was my first meal in America. I could never forget this first meal and the funny adventures associated with it. I will cherish this experience forever.

The next morning, we got our first cultural shock at the YMCA hostel. We were not used to taking communal showers without any clothes. We were shocked to see the guests walking from their rooms to the shower— naked—and showering in communal, open shower stalls (without any curtains). For a while, we tried to avoid other people in the shower room, which was not possible. Finally, we got the courage to do the same.

We were not familiar with the local bus system. We walked from the downtown YMCA to the IIT campus, almost six miles. Once we were on campus, we met with the mechanical engineering chair and the foreign student adviser. They provided all the information and help we needed. We were low on pocket funds. Our funds for tuition fees and living expenses were payable to IIT, because of the Government of India's policy. We opened our individual checking accounts and received some cash for pocket expenses. The foreign student adviser also made temporary arrangements for us to stay in the IIT dorm and taught us how to use the local bus and train systems. We took the bus back to the YMCA, checked out, and moved our luggage into the dorm room.

We knew we could neither afford to live in the dorm nor get used to the dorm food. We looked for an apartment in the nearby area. We met an old and kind lady who owned a real estate office right across from the IIT campus (on the other side of Interstate 94). She rented us a three-bedroom apartment above her office at 3038 Wentworth Street. The place was old and was situated next to a dry-cleaning plant, but it was within walking distance from the campus. It was in a very run-down area. We did not know anything about that at that time. To us, everything looked excellent. We moved into the apartment. The landlady helped us to get our apartment furnished. She gave us three study tables, a sofa, and a dining table. Her helper took us to a Salvation Army store. We bought used beds from the store. We three moved to the apartment from the dorm. In a few days, three other Indian students also moved in with us. We all six were sharing the three-bedroom apartment. We started cooking our meals. This arrangement brought our lodging and boarding costs below fifty dollars a month.

By this time, I had recovered from the homesickness and started worrying about my studies. However, there were a few incidents that made me homesick for a brief period, and I thought about returning to India. I heard that a few homesick foreign students had returned home within a month. I did not want to be in that statistic. I had no other choice but to continue my studies.

5.2 POSTGRADUATE EDUCATION AT ILLINOIS INSTITUTE OF TECHNOLOGY, CHICAGO, ILLINOIS (SEPTEMBER 1963–DECEMBER 1964)

As soon we had settled down in the apartment, the schooling started at full speed. I had to learn many new things in addition to the coursework, such as the course selection and registration process (in India, I had to take a fixed set of courses), understanding lecturers and fellow students, teaching

Figure 5.1: Student at the Illinois Institute of Technology.

44

styles, homework, the grading system, evening classes, open-book exams, take-home exams, being on time, etc.

It was a difficult start, but I got the hang of them quickly, and I started getting good grades. I took eighteen credit hours in the first semester. However, I had to drop out of computer programming. I had not been exposed to computers at all. I could not understand the logic behind the programming languages. Later on, I understood the logic, took it again, and passed it. I completed the courses required for the MSME degree in two semesters. I had to complete my thesis to graduate. This required a summer semester. I wrote a thesis under Professor Kalpakjain called "Changes in Properties of Metals due to Mechanical Working." I defended my thesis in December 1964 and got accepted. I graduated with my MSME in January 1965 with a 3.77 GPA.

During this period, I learned a lot about American culture. I made a few good American friends. As a foreign student, I was invited to celebrate Thanksgiving with an American family, Dr. and Mrs. Elghammer, in Danville, Illinois, as detailed in chapter 14.5. I enjoyed their hospitality, respect, and dedication to foreign students. This was my first exposure to an upper-middle-class American family with small children living in a small town. I learned a lot from this visit. Similarly, I celebrated my first Christmas with another family in Evanston, Illinois. They also welcomed me into their family and gave me gifts.

Right after school started, I got part-time work on campus as a grader and graduate assistant. This job generated enough income for my living expenses. Because of this job, I did not need any more funds from India. I became self-supporting again and relieved my parents of the financial burden.

While working as a grader and graduate assistant at IIT, I developed a close relationship with Professor R. A. Budenholzer. I conducted his classes when he had to go out of town for some emergencies. His secretary helped me to type and edit my thesis. Professor Budenholzer helped me get my first engineering job with Foster Wheeler (see chapter 7.1).

5.3 ROUGH PERIOD LOOKING FOR A JOB

I completed the needed coursework and started working on my thesis at the end of the second semester. I got a summer job as a lab technician in the IIT aerodynamics lab. As soon as the summer semester was over, the first draft of my thesis was ready for review. I knew that defending my thesis would happen later in the fall semester and that I would graduate with the MSME degree in January 1965. This gave me ample time to look for a job.

I started sending résumés to any organization that was hiring mechanical engineers. That did not produce any results. I went to Milwaukee, Wisconsin, to visit potential employers personally. That didn't produce any results. Then I went to Detroit, Michigan; Akron, Ohio; and Cleveland, Ohio. I didn't have money to stay in a hotel, so I had to stay with friends. They were kind to feed me and let me stay for free in their living rooms. I didn't have a car to visit potential employers. I either took public transportation or just walked from the nearest public transportation stop. After two weeks of intensive job searching, nothing materialized. That was heartbreaking. I was running low on money. I didn't want to ask for more money from my parents. I got very discouraged and depressed. I felt very helpless. I didn't know what to do. I thought American companies were discriminating. This was one of the most troubling periods of my life. When I came to the promised land of America, I had dreams of getting an advanced degree in mechanical engineering and working for a reputable, well-known company. But those dreams were not realized.

Finally, with the help of an employment agency, I got a very low, entry-level job with a small company that manufactured sheet metal cutting tools in the Chicago area. I had no choice but to take it.

5.4 FIRST JOB AT F. J. LITTELL MACHINE COMPANY, CHICAGO, ILLINOIS

My job at the F. J. Little Machine Company was to find spare parts for their machine tools in the field. Later, they started giving me drafting jobs. This company was running a tightfisted operation. There was lots of overtime with little pay. They needed neither my engineering skills nor my degree. When I gave some ideas for improvements, the chief engineer snubbed me. They wanted me to remain as a draftsman only. I had no choice but to stick around until I could find a better job. This was my first job in the real-world industry. I kept learning business operation systems and etiquette. One good thing that came out of this job was learning to drive. One of my fellow employees was attending junior college and was taking calculus. He had a hard time doing assignments and passing exams. I helped him with calculus, and he taught me to drive.

I was commuting to the company from my apartment, near the IIT campus, which took over an hour by bus. I moved closer to the workplace and lived with an Indian friend, Ashok Desai, at 927 Belle Plane.

I worked for this company for less than nine months. I made enough money to repay my debt in India. I left the job as soon as I found a good engineering job at a reputable company.

In October 1964, I sent five thousand rupees to India, my first paycheck, to my parents. I told them to use this money for their pilgrimage to wherever they wanted to go in India. They were touched by my love and dedication to them. They went on the pilgrimage with pride and satisfaction. I felt exceptionally good about it. My father kept telling me about their pilgrimage whenever I visited him. Unfortunately, my mother did not survive to tell me about her joy in person.

6

GETTING A COMPLEMENTARY LIFE PARTNER

As soon as I moved away from campus, I started feeling a void in my life. I felt a need for a complementary life partner to establish roots, grow, and blossom in the transplanted land. Until now, I had never given any serious thought to it. Earlier, I'd thought about it but never followed up with any action. To get one of my choices, I had to overcome several family traditions, Patidar community customs, and social hurdles. As described in the following sections, it took little time to persuade everyone involved in the process.

6.1 OLD CUSTOMS

When I was growing up, Indian families had to abide by the rigid social customs of marrying a partner within the same caste. This meant that I must marry a girl from the Kadwa Patel caste only. Also, most of the men's and women's matches were arranged by the parents and/or family members. If this custom was continued when I was ready to look for a life partner, I might not have had any choice but to select a life partner whom my parents had selected for me. Fortunately, the customs started getting a little permissive with society's modernization and education.

Starting from the early sixties, a few families let their kids select his/her own life partner. My parents indicated that they would welcome whomever

I select as my life partner, from the Kadwa Patel caste. Also, some families had the guts to go for intercaste marriage. Our family did not have that courage. Neither did I. Among my circle of relatives and friends, only one person had the guts to marry a girl from another caste in 1964. I did not dare to do that. I was afraid that my parents and close relatives would not approve of my marrying a girl from another caste. I did not want to hurt their feelings.

6.2 CHILDHOOD ENGAGEMENT

When I was a child, our Kadwa Patel community had a very weird and impractical religious/social custom. All the weddings of the community members were held in the designated year. The religious leaders designated the year only once every twelve years. To abide by the custom, most unmarried boys and girls, irrespective of age, got married during that year. If you missed getting married during the designated year, you had to wait up to twelve years. Before the designated year arrived, all the unmarried boys and girls, irrespective of age, would find their matches (with the help of their parents and/or relatives), get engaged, and wait. This custom forced them to get engaged soon after birth, at an early age.

I was a victim of the above custom. When I was about two years old, one of my cousin's relatives had a girl. After her birth, my cousin arranged for my engagement with the newly born girl. I was engaged to her when I was two years old.

Her name was Mukta. I had never met her. I did not know anything about her. Whenever I met my cousin, she used to talk about her. I did not pay any attention to that. My parents sent her some jewelry on a few occasions. When I was four years old, the mass wedding custom was abolished and discontinued. However, my engagement with Mukta continued until I was in the ninth grade. At that time, her parents requested that my parents either set a wedding date immediately or call off the engagement. My father and I decided to call off my childhood engagement.

6.3 Early Thoughts and Choices for a Complementary Life Partner

I was raised in a very ordinary farmer's family with very little education and exposure to the modern world. I attended a boys-only elementary school, middle school, and high school. I never saw, talked to, or socialized with any schoolgirls of my age and my liking. I had no idea what to look for in a life partner.

In my family, none of my elder sisters, aunts, cousin-sisters, or sisters-in-law had any formal education. That did not give me any guidelines for looking for a life partner. I never knew any college-educated ladies until I met Mr. and Mrs. Velankar in 1957 when I was in the eleventh grade (see chapter 9.5). Since they both were college graduates and broad-minded from cultured families, I learned a lot from both.

The most valuable and important thing they helped with was what I should be looking for in my future life partner by giving me a rare opportunity to socialize with his younger sister, Manda. This was my first experience meeting an educated and cultured girl of my age, and it occurred during the vacation of 1958 when I was waiting for the SSC Board Exam results and Mr. Velankar's family (his elder sister, younger sister Manda, and younger brother) visited him in Shapur.

Manda and I had many things in common such as the following: (i) we had both just completed high school and were waiting for our SSC Board Exam results; (ii) we were getting ready to start college life, the next phase of our lives, and were preparing to live an independent life in a college dormitory; (iii) we both liked math and science; and (iv) we both were smart students and were getting excellent grades. Because of our similarities, Mr. Velankar asked me to be her host to show her around town, bring her to places of interest, and keep her company. This included their family trip to Climb mount Girnar in Junagadh, a two-day trip of ten thousand steps to climb.

This socialization event widened my horizon, and I overcame the barrier and fear. I learned how to socialize freely with a cultured and modern girl of my age. Mr. Velankar gave us the freedom to socialize without any supervision. (At that time, it was taboo in our society.) Our paths never crossed again. We both got busy with our college study goals. Mr. Velankar kept me informed about her progress in college. She gained admission into medical school and became a doctor.

This was a rare learning opportunity that gave me ideas on what to look for in my future life partner.

Once I finished undergraduate engineering college, I became very busy with making final preparations for my travel to America for graduate study. I had to raise funds (borrow money) for travel and study expenses, get a student visa, book travel, attend receptions and orientation, complete the last-minute shopping, and arrange for money transfers. Occupied with these activities, I never seriously thought about getting married before going to America. It was not on my list of priorities. Since I had many important things to take care of before leaving for America, I decided to continue my preparations without getting married.

Four months before I left for America, Mrs. Velankar asked me a direct question about whether I would be interested in pursuing a relationship with Manda. If I was, she would be ready to help. I thought about her question for a while. I liked Manda, but I was not ready to get married before going to America, as described in the previous paragraph.

While I was busy with my preparations, my cousin-sister Labhuben's relative's daughter, Manju, (from Mumbai) was visiting her uncle in Upleta, only forty miles from my hometown of Shapur. My uncle Jasmat and my cousin-sister insisted that I should take advantage of her visit to a nearby city and just meet her. I had no choice but to abide by their wish. With a little reluctance, but with an open mind, I agreed to meet Manju at her uncle's (Chunikaka) place in Upleta, as detailed in the following section.

6.4 Meeting Manju for the First Time

Since my cousin Labhuben's husband was related to Manju's parents, living in the same Mumbai neighborhood, she had known Manju since her childhood. She had remarkably high regard for Manju and her parents. Whenever I met Labhuben, she always talked about Manju and her good nature and educational and extracurricular achievements. I never paid too much attention. She was telling me indirectly that Manju was the right girl for me. Up to that time, I had known about Manju only what I had been told. On the other side, when I went to college and started talking about going to engineering college in America, she was impressed by my achievements (I was the first one to go to college in our family), and she told good things about me to Manju and her parents. By the time we met for the first time, we knew a little bit about each other. Manju did meet my most important criteria for a life partner: she would be a college-educated life partner.

With this background, I was looking forward to meeting her in person. Meeting Manju became a well-organized event arranged by our families. It was a traditional event: a boy meets a girl at a family house. They are given a few minutes of privacy to talk. I met Manju at her uncle's place on May 24, 1963, in Upleta. This was my only experience meeting an adult girl for matrimony purposes. In the short time given to us, Manju and I talked about my plans to go to America and her willingness to join me if I decided to marry her. I liked her and developed some feelings for her. This meeting was to meet and see each other and talk, but no touching or hugging was allowed. However, considering other family factors and there being no time for marriage, I had already decided not to get married before leaving India. She was disappointed by my decision. She made a last-minute appeal for a quick marriage during my last week in India. I had to reject her appeal because I was preoccupied with my final preparations before leaving India. However, I told her, "I like you, and I have good feelings for you. I would like to continue our acquaintance/friendship by staying in touch, and I will consider marrying you whenever I will come back." I also met her at Labhuben's home the day before I departed from India and told her the same thing. At that time, she could not accept my suggestion to stay in touch and continue the relationship. Once I arrived in America, I got busy with my studies, and marriage became a secondary issue. However, I wanted to keep my relationship live with Manju, so I wrote her once, a small note in my letter to Labhuben, wishing her the best of luck with her BA (bachelor of arts) degree examination. The intention was to give my current contact information. She never replied to my note. I assumed that she had gotten married and was gone. I was wrong.

6.5 ENGAGEMENT WITH MANJU

I started feeling lonely when I finished my thesis at IIT and moved away from the active social life at the IIT campus and into an apartment. It was near my workplace, in north Chicago. My roommate was either working overtime or going out with his girlfriend. I often stayed alone in our new apartment. He pressured me a lot to go out with local girls. He was willing to help me find girls. I resisted the pressure. That wasn't my way of finding a complementary life partner. But at the same time, I didn't know what to do. There was nobody with whom I felt comfortable talking about my problem. I was in a dilemma. At this point in my life, I knew only two girls: Majnu and Manda, as described in the previous sections. They both met my criteria for a life partner. When I met them, I was not ready to get married. Now I was ready, but I neither knew about their current marital status nor how to approach them. While I was suffering from this troubling dilemma, I received a letter from Manju in early January 1965. What a lucky break!

When I reflect on her letter, a few questions arise. What inspired her to write the letter at that time? Did she know about my troubling situation? Was this my stroke of luck, or some telepathy? Whatever the answer might have been, it didn't matter to me. I was ready to restart our relationship communication.

Manju wrote the letter in the name of her sister Sharda, stating that Manju wanted to continue dialogue with me for her marriage. The timing of her letter was just right. As mentioned above, I was lonely and wanted a complementary life partner. I replied, and we rekindled our feelings by mail. After exchanging a few letters, I decided to marry her. She welcomed my decision. We told our parents about our decision to get married. They welcomed and supported our decision and started preparations for our engagement. Manju and her family traveled to Upleta for our engagement ceremony. I got engaged in absentia on May 27, 1965, at Manju's uncle's place in Upleta where we met for the first time. After our engagement, Manju visited my family in Shapur. She was the first educated (college graduate) daughter-in-law in the Dhudshia family. All the family members were taking pride in having Manju in the Dhudshia family, especially, my mother, father, and uncle Jasmat.

Right after my engagement to Manju, I got the first mechanical engineering job of my preference, with a reputable corporation, the Foster Wheeler Corporation, in Livingston, New Jersey. I felt that my luck had changed with my engagement with Manju. Not only that, but my parents also felt the same way. They told me that Lakshmi (the goddess of wealth) had come into my life.

Now the question was about marriage. I had neither the money nor the vacation time for a trip to India. I found out that I could sponsor her to visit America on a fiancée's visa. I was not sure that Manju would agree with my suggestion for her to come to America. For her, it was taking a big chance. However, she trusted my suggestion and agreed to travel to America to get married.

As soon as I settled down at the Ivy Hill Apartments in Newark, New Jersey, I started the paperwork for Manju to get a visa, as my fiancée, to come to America. It was much easier than I had thought. She got her visa in August 1965. I made reservations for her travel and sent a ticket for her trip to America.

6.6 MANJU'S ARRIVAL IN AMERICA (SEPTEMBER 19, 1965)

September 19, 1965 was an important day of my life. It was going to change significantly, starting on that day. Until that time, I had lived a single life, either alone or with other male friends in dorms or apartments. Today it was going to end. I was going to get a life partner, and we were going to grow and thrive together in the transplanted land, and I would share everything I had for the rest of my life.

In the early morning, I started cleaning my apartment and arranging and rearranging my stuff. I called Air India and confirmed that Manju was on the flight, and my heart started beating faster. Only a few hours remained before I would meet her in a different situation. My friends Vallabh Patel and Kumar Kalola came with me to the John F. Kennedy International Airport to receive her. The flight arrived right on time. I watched her, from the receiving lounge, going through immigration and customs. Now was the moment to welcome her into my life. My friends challenged me to hug her. I hugged her, and it was the first time I had ever touched her. We took a little stroll around the airport before going to the car.

Once we arrived at our apartment, we exchanged rings and became life partners. There was neither any ceremony nor any celebration. We spent the rest of the day catching up on whatever we had missed since our last meeting on August 18, 1963.

Figure 6.1: Marrying Manju.

6.7 MARRYING MANJU

After her arrival in America, we applied for the marriage license and made other preparations for our wedding. Since there was no licensed Hindu priest to perform the marriage ceremony, we got married in court on October 1, 1965, and followed up with a Hindu ceremony, performed (using a Hindu wedding instruction book) by a longtime engineer friend, Mahesh Dixit, on October 3, 1965.

Our wedding was an atypical Indian wedding. Normally, it is a two- or three-day process that includes putting on henna, *garba* (folk dancing), a grandiose groom's arrival, a wedding ceremony on the decorated stage, a stately reception, and an emotional goodbye to the bride. Our wedding was in the social room in the Ivy Hill Apartment's basement (simply decorated by our friends). It was comprised of a basic, short, and simple Hindu wedding ceremony. The follow-up reception was also quite simple. At that time, there were no Indian food caterers. Manju and our friends prepared Indian food for the reception. Some of my close friends living in the New York and New Jersey areas, and my coworkers from the Foster Wheeler Corporation, attended our wedding. None of our relatives could attend the wedding. Since there were no relatives from either side at our wedding, we both felt their absence. For our honeymoon, we went to Niagara Falls with our friend Kantilal Kalaria.

I was the first one to invite a fiancée, on a special fiancée's visa, from India to America and the first to get married this way in America.

Manju had to cross several cultural divides between us, like: (i) several of her close relatives were highly educated, I had only one; (ii) her family was living in a big city, my family was a farming family living in a small town; (iii) she grew up as a city girl in a big, cosmopolitan city, while I was a village boy, and so forth. However, she was educated and open-minded. That made her flexible to adapt to changing circumstances.

As described in the following chapters, having an educated, open-minded, complementary, supportive, hardworking, and loving life partner made our journey together fulfilling through various phases of our lives. Our union resulted in having a successful and self-satisfying life together in the transplanted land.

7

PUTTING ROOTS DEEPER IN THE TRANSPLANTED LAND

7.1 WORKING LIFE AT FOSTER WHEELER CORPORATION (JUNE 1965–SEPTEMBER 1972)

I was not happy with my job with the F. J. Littell Machine Company in Chicago. As soon as I received my MSME degree, I started looking for a better job. I got a job at Foster Wheeler in a very unusual way. I requested Professor R. A. Budenholzer, for whom I worked as a grader and graduate assistant at IIT, to help me find a job within his circle. He knew the chief executive officer (CEO) of the Foster Wheeler Corporation, in Livingston, New Jersey, who had been his student. He gave me a letter of recommendation to take to him when I visited Livingston. At that time, I did not know anything about the CEO's position and authority. When I went to the Foster Wheeler Corporation's headquarters, I told the receptionist, "I want to see Mr. Thompson." She asked me why I wanted to see him. I told her, " He was Professor Budenholzer's student, and I have a letter for him." She took my letter to him. Within a few minutes, he came out and introduced himself. We chatted briefly about Professor Budenholzer, and then he took me to the HR manager and told him that Foster Wheeler must offer me a job today, and then he left. I had an interview immediately and a job offer within a few hours. At that time, I did not know that I was being helped by the CEO. I never met him again. After I started working for Foster Wheeler, I realized who he was and why I had been given the job so quickly.

My first assignment at Foster Wheeler (FW), as a specialist engineer in design engineering, was to model and calculate stresses in power plant components, mostly boilers and heat exchangers. My group consisted of five engineers and a manager, Ed Edwards, an incredibly soft-spoken and caring gentleman. I developed good friendships and working relationships with all my coworkers. All of them attended my wedding.

At that time, electronic calculators were unheard of. I used a Monroe mechanical calculator (which was the size of a typewriter) for my calculations. Later, I got an electronic calculator with tubes. I learned computer programs for piping analysis for power and chemical plants. This included calculations for stress due to shocks and vibrations. The theoretical calculations were verified by actual shock testing of the power plant components.

After working for five years in design engineering, I switched to FW's research center as a research engineer. I worked on flow-induced vibrations in the nuclear heat exchanger's tube bank. This included theoretical calculations and testing of engineering models. Later, I took a challenging assignment to understand and interpret the reliability requirements for the nuclear heat exchanger that FW was going to build. This assignment was the beginning of my interest in the reliability discipline. I learned a lot by myself about reliability. Later, I chose reliability as my major for my PhD.

Working for Foster Wheeler was a great opportunity to sharpen my technical skills, work among highly educated coworkers, and get an advanced degree. Not only that, but I also made many good friends for life. Among them were Dr. P. K. Patel, Dr. P. D. Patel, Marty Bernstein, Dr. A. C. Gangadharan, and Dr. Harold Levy.

7.2 GETTING DOCTORATE DEGREE AT NEW YORK UNIVERSITY

During the second year of my employment with Foster Wheeler, I noticed that some of my coworkers were going to school part-time for further study.

Foster Wheeler encouraged such study by giving time off and paying for tuition and books. I took advantage of such generous benefits and joined a branch of New York University, in the Bronx, New York, for my PhD on a part-time basis. I started with courses in engineering statistics, quality control, and reliability. In the beginning, I took a public bus from the Ivy Hill Apartments to Port Authority Terminal in New York and then took the subway to the Bronx campus. It used to be a long journey. When I mastered driving, I started driving to the campus, almost fifty miles one way. When I completed the required courses, I took and passed a qualifying exam for my PhD. Now the only thing that remained was the thesis. I was in a dilemma about whether to continue with my PhD. The country was going through a recession, and nobody was hiring PhDs. After procrastinating for six months, I found a topic by a fluke while working on my homework for an advanced reliability course. Professor Dubey liked the topic, and he agreed to become an adviser for my thesis. With the help of computer programmers, working in the Foster Wheeler research group, and using the Foster Wheeler Corporation's computer, I cranked out lots of data for my thesis during the Christmas vacation in 1971. Professor Dubey was impressed with the results, and he asked me to start writing my thesis. The first draft of my thesis was ready by May 1972. While I was still working on my final draft, Xerox Corporation advertised a job that matched my interest and background perfectly. Without being serious, I applied for the position. Immediately I had an interview with them and received a job offer. I was not sure about leaving my career at the Foster Wheeler Corporation, but the Xerox job looked more interesting, challenging, and promising. I accepted the Xerox offer.

Once I started the Xerox job, I completed the final draft of my thesis and defended it in March 1973. I received my PhD on June 11, 1973, at Madison Square Garden Arena in New York City. Manju and Neha attended the ceremony.

Figure 7.1: Getting PhD at NYU, May, 1973.

7.3 WORKING LIFE AT XEROX CORPORATION (SEPTEMBER 1972–APRIL 1984)

A. Computer Printer Division

I started my career with the Xerox Corporation as an engineering specialist in the newly created Computer Printer Division in Rochester, New York, on September 5, 1972. The division was created by combining Xerox's core technology with computer technology.

My hiring supervisor was Dr. John Bessley, a Britain-raised and educated gentleman. He liked my unique combination of mechanical engineering and reliability engineering skills. He was kind and helpful. Since I switched industries, from power plant components to computer printers, I had a lot to learn. It did not take me that long to get up the speed. Initially, I worked on two versions of the Xerox computer printer: Xerox 1200 and Xerox 5700. After I worked in Rochester for about a year, Xerox moved the printer lines to Dallas, Texas, on Mockingbird Lane. I had to move to Dallas, like many other Xerox employees working on computer printers. When we moved to the Dallas area, we bought a house in Plano, Texas, and we have lived in Plano ever since.

After our move to Dallas, Dr. John Bessley got the promotion and became a second-level manager. Bhogin Modi, a longtime Xerox employee, became my immediate manager. My job objective was to improve the reliability of the computer printers. I had to work with design, manufacturing, field engineers, and a program manager. My duties included design assessment, reliability testing, field performance tracking, running a failure review board, tracking the status of the corrective actions, and projecting future performance.

B. Inkjet Printer Development Group

When the Computer Printer Division was transferred to El Segundo, California, I decided to stay in Dallas and took a position in the inkjet printer development group as a development engineer. Xerox was successful in developing the inkjet technology but was not able to mass-produce the maintenance-free inkjet heads cheaply. After a while, Xerox decided to discontinue the inkjet development program and transferred all the employees to other groups in Dallas, Texas.

C. Office Product Manufacturing Group

When the inkjet development program was discontinued, I was transferred to the Office Product Manufacturing Group as a quality planning and analysis manager. In that group, I worked for Cecilia Craig, a nice and very career-oriented lady. I had a staff of two engineers and two technicians. My group tracked the quality data from the product lines and performed quality audits. I also provided quality and reliability training to manufacturing engineers. In mid-1983, Xerox decided to close Dallas manufacturing operations and offered me a job in other Xerox locations. I had to choose between El Segundo, California; Fremont, California; and Rochester, New York. I did not like any one of the locations. I chose the volunteer layoff alternative with a good benefits package. This was the end of my career with Xerox.

Xerox was a very employee-friendly company with creativity-inspiring employee benefits. There were lots of learning and advancement opportunities. I am grateful to my supervisors, Dr. John Bessley and Mr. Bhogin Modi, for giving me the freedom to be creative.

7.4 IN BETWEEN XEROX CORPORATION AND TEXAS INSTRUMENTS INC.

Since Xerox gave me a good benefits package for taking a volunteer layoff, I tried my luck in a business of my own. I bought a partnership with Pecunia Inc., which owned Century 21 and V. R. Business Brokers franchises. I obtained a real estate broker's license and became a comanager with Robert Swartz. We moved to a bigger office and increased the staff. After being with the group, I found out that Robert Swartz was engaged in illegal transactions and was siphoning off revenues from our office revenue. I exposed him to the silent partners. Our three partners bought his partnership shares and let him go. I became the chief office manager, managing the Century 21 office and supervising the V. R. Business Brokers office manager. The office manager was solving mostly personal problems. It did not give me any technical stimulation. I started getting bored. After a while, I found out that it was not my cup of tea. While working as chief office manager, I took a part-time job with the University of Texas at Arlington, as an adjunct professor teaching engineering statistics. At the same time, the tax laws changed, which gave fewer benefits to real estate investors. This affected our sales, which went down significantly. For some months, we could not even cover our fixed office expenses. An opportunity to get out of this business came around. One of my real estate agents sold twelve very old houses to a real estate developer for commercial use. We got a big commission check. Soon after that, we gave away the Century 21 office and its franchise rights to our agent, free and clear. I started managing only the V. R. Business Brokers office.

While I was managing the V. R. Business Brokers office and teaching at the University of Texas at Arlington, I got a call from Texas Instruments for a consultation to help them improve the reliability of their process equipment. I took the consulting job. Within a month, Texas Instruments was impressed by my unique skill set (mechanical and reliability engineering) and made me an offer for a full-time job, which I could not resist. I sold the V. R. Business Brokers office, and I got out of running the brokerage business. After spending three years in the brokerage business, I went back to a technical career.

7.5 WORKING LIFE AT TEXAS INSTRUMENTS INC. (1986–2001)

A. Process Automation Center (PAC) Division

As mentioned in the last section, my career with Texas Instruments (TI) started early in 1986 when I started working as a contract reliability engineer for TI's Process Automation Center (PAC) Division. At that time,

I was managing V. R. Business Brokers and teaching at the University of Texas at Arlington. Working as a consultant, I prepared a road map for improving the reliability of the PAC product lines. Once the road map was ready, PAC management liked it, but they did not have anyone to implement it. TI offered me an attractive permanent position. Immediately, I and my Pecunia Inc. partners sold the brokerage business, and I accepted the permanent job with TI as a reliability assurance manager for the PAC product lines.

My reliability assurance group helped the TI PAC Division to improve the reliability of the process equipment, manufactured by the TI PAC Division and currently in operation in the TI manufacturing facilities. My reliability group also helped to design-in reliability in the new generations of equipment. As a result of my group's efforts, the reliability of PAC products improved three- to fourfold in a short time. However, it became apparent in 1990 that TI PAC could not compete with large semiconductor manufacturing equipment suppliers like Lam Research and Applied Materials. The PAC Division started losing high-level management support. Before TI abandoned the PAC Division and sold, I was given an opportunity to go to SEMATECH, as detailed in the following Section.

B. SEMATECH Assignment (1991–1994)

In early 1991, Ben Sloan, VP of the PAC Division, arranged for me to go to SEMATECH (semiconductor manufacturing technology), a research consortium of American semiconductor manufacturers and the Department of Defense (DOD). SEMATECH was created to improve the competitive position of American semiconductor manufacturers and manufacturing equipment suppliers. This was a rare opportunity for me to represent TI, as a TI assignee, in the consortium with assignees from IBM, Intel, National Semiconductor, Motorola, AMD, AT&T, and others. I managed a group of reliability engineers providing support to semiconductor manufacturing equipment suppliers to improve the reliability of their products. I also managed reliability improvement programs contracted to Sandia National Laboratories in Albuquerque, New Mexico. Our group developed guidelines for equipment reliability, failure reporting and corrective action systems (FRACAS), failure mode and effect analysis (FMEA), etc. I also developed: (i) a course on equipment reliability overview for nonreliability professionals, engineers, and their managers; and (ii) a course on guidelines for designing in reliability. I taught both courses several times at major semiconductor manufacturing-related symposiums. The teaching helped me to improve both courses a lot. Later, I used the course material to author a book, in 1995, titled *Hi-Tech Equipment Reliability*. The publication of my book gave a big boost to my name recognition in the semiconductor manufacturing sector as Mr. Reliability.

While at SEMATECH, I did a lot of researching and studying about equipment reliability. These self-driven efforts gave me a complete vision of equipment reliability which included its practical measures, its application to real-life situations, and its application to equipment program life-cycle phases (design development phase through the maturity phase). When I started working at SEMATECH, the semiconductor industry used several equipment performance metrics. They all looked scattered and disjointed. I tied them together with a hierarchy tree. My equipment performance metrics hierarchy chart became one of the most popular and useful charts in the semiconductor industry. Some of the users called the chart the Dhudshia Equipment Performance Metrics Hierarchy Chart. The hierarchy chart is one of the key highlights of my book. I have given several copyright permissions to use it in various publications.

My years at SEMATECH were the best years of my career. I was more creative and productive. The working environment at SEMATECH was very conducive to creativity. There was no limit on the budget. I could travel anywhere, attend any symposium/seminar, and contract with anyone for consulting. While working in this environment, I learned a lot and made many friends. I had opportunities to visit the wafer fabs of most of the SEMATECH members. I felt very satisfied that I was able to contribute to improving the competitive position of American semiconductor manufacturers and the manufacturing equipment suppliers. As a result of SEMATECH's efforts, the American semiconductor industry turned around and regained its competitive position. I am happy to be one of the contributors to the turnaround.

I was one of the few lucky employees who got a once-in-a-lifetime chance to represent TI, as an assignee, at SEMATECH.

The only bad part of the SEMATECH assignment was that I had to live in Austin, Texas, on weekdays. I lived in an apartment near SEMATECH on weekdays and commuted back to Dallas on weekends. This took me away from family. Manju had to manage the day-to-day family and home affairs. This was a different lifestyle for me. I learned to live by myself on frozen food care packages from home. I enjoyed living in Austin, Texas, particularly jogging around Lake Austin.

C. Manufacturing Science and Technology Center (MSTC) Job (1994–1995)

When I came back from SEMATECH to TI in January 1994, I joined the equipment QRA group under Dan Joseph in TI's Manufacturing Science and Technology Center (MSTC). There I continued helping TI's four key equipment suppliers (Applied Materials, KLA-Tencor, Canon, and Tokyo Electron) to improve the quality and reliability of their products in TI fabs. I tracked their performance, provided feedback, performed standardized supplier quality assessment (SSQA) audits, provided equipment reliability training, and gave SEMI E10 specification consulting support. When my book, *Hi-Tech Equipment Reliability*, was published in 1995, I provided reliability training to TI engineers and managers worldwide. The publication of my book gave a big boost to my technical career. I became a well-known expert in equipment reliability in the semiconductor industry. I received many invitations to give talks, training, and seminars within TI and outside TI worldwide. TI promoted me on the technical ladder as a senior member of the technical staff. The American Society for Quality (ASQ) awarded me a fellowship of the society. Considering the reader base is limited to the semiconductor industry, my book sales were good. I did not become rich from the book royalties; however, they gave me a big morale boost and a nickname as Mr. Reliability.

D. Worldwide Procurement and Logistics (WPL) Job (1995–2001)

When MSTC got integrated with TI's development K-Fab, our QRA group became a part of the Worldwide Procurement and Logistics (WPL) group. When Dan Joseph got laid off, I became a technical staff member of the WPL, reporting directly to a second-level manager named Rob Simpson. I continue supporting and evaluating suppliers. I worked a little more closely with TI's key suppliers to improve their business process for QRA. I also helped TI to improve the reliability data tracking system based on SEMI E10 specifications. As a result, the key suppliers' performances improved significantly. I was invited to write a chapter on equipment reliability in the *Semiconductor Manufacturing Technology Handbook*, sponsored by TI with contributions from technical experts from all over TI. This was one more opportunity for me to get recognized as an equipment reliability expert.

Once the TI equipment suppliers achieved an excellent level in meeting TI's quality and reliability requirements, TI started changing the support level for them. Slowly, TI shifted the QRA responsibility to the suppliers. This made my function less important. I knew that, when a bad time would come, my position would be eliminated. I tried to switch to other groups. Before I could do that, the entire high-tech industry went south. That triggered layoffs all over the semiconductor manufacturing industry. Since I had been recognized just two months before as a valuable contributor to the WPL group, I hoped that I would survive the downturn. I was wrong.

E. Abrupt End

On the morning of April 25, 2001, I started my workday at TI as usual. I reviewed my mail, emails, and messages. Before I answered them, my immediate supervisor came into my office and closed the door. I knew something bad was going to happen! He presented me with my layoff papers, requested to surrender my employee badge and office key, and asked me to collect my personal items. He helped me to put them in a box and carried them to my car. Once I put my stuff in my car, my supervisor left me without saying anything, except wishing me good luck.

As I sat in my car, I was totally dumbfounded. This unexpected event gave me a big shock. I was trembling. I couldn't comprehend what had just happened to me. I sat in my car for a while, completely thoughtless. I didn't know what to do next. I felt hopeless and helpless. After sitting in such a condition for more than fifteen minutes, I collected myself and started my car.

Since this was the last time I would see Mother TI, I drove in a circle around the TI campus, with my heart pounding and tears in my eyes. It was a very emotional circle. I had run hundreds of times around the TI campus at lunchtime for physical exercise. But this last circle in my car was different. I felt like I was going away from my mother (TI), as I did thirty-eight years earlier when I had left my mother (Ganga) in India.

When I came home, no one was at home. Everything looked bleak. I didn't know what to tell my family and friends. I became depressed and isolated.

Getting this involuntary layoff was a demoralizing experience in my life. I could not comprehend how the corporate world worked. After giving fifteen years of my life as a very honest, hardworking, and dedicated employee who never took time off for sickness and always put TI's interests first, the relationship had ended in a flash.

In a few days, it sank in and I accepted working in the American corporate world. This helped me to recover from the shock and depression and regain my sanity.

When I reflect on this time, I feel that I was fortunate, and I'm glad that my employment with TI had lasted almost fifteen years. During that time, my career in reliability blossomed. I am grateful to my supervisors for giving me the freedom to be creative. I am also grateful for TI's creativity-inspiring employee benefits policy. During this period, I was encouraged and allowed to: (i) meet many experts in equipment reliability, (ii) attend seminars and symposiums related to equipment reliability all over the world, (iii) promote equipment reliability within TI and the semiconductor manufacturing equipment industry, and finally, (iv) publish my book.

On top of all that, I am grateful to TI for giving me a once-in-a-lifetime opportunity to represent TI at SEMATECH, which was the most creative two years of my career. Also, it gave me the self-satisfaction of contributing to improving the competitive position of American semiconductor manufacturers and the manufacturing equipment suppliers.

When my employment ended with TI, I was well settled in my transplanted land of America. My financial condition was strong. Our house was fully paid for, and there were no other debts. My kids had finished their educations and were well-placed in the professions of their choice. I had great name recognition in the semiconductor manufacturing industry. These favorable conditions helped me to weather the shock of the abrupt end of my employment with TI. I was ready to go on with life on my own, as described in the following section.

7.6 WELL-ESTABLISHED, MATURE TRANSPLANTED MAN

My layoff in early 2001 was very ill-timed. The American industry got into the worst down cycle it had ever experienced. It was just coming out from the downturn, and then the September 11 attack on the World Trade Center happened. That devastated the entire American economy. Its repercussions went way beyond the World Trade Center. The stock market took a dive, and more people got laid off in the high-tech industry. At the same time, my age started becoming a factor in getting a job. I had many interviews and prospects for jobs. Once they found out that I was reaching my sixty-fifth birthday, they did not offer me any job. I started experiencing age discrimination. I was unable to do anything about that.

A. Consulting to the Semiconductor Industry

There were many ex-TIers, like me, who were not ready to retire fully. They all were looking to do something in their field of expertise. Luckily, I ran into an ex-TIer named Carl Williams, who was starting a consulting firm. He invited me to join the firm, SafeFab Solutions, as an associate.

After I joined SafeFab Solutions, I started getting some jobs in 2001 and early 2002. Finally, I got a good break with Applied Materials Inc., with help from Mr. Surinder Bedi, manager of global quality and reliability. He was a longtime follower of my book and my methodology for improving equipment reliability and quality. I developed material for a customized worldwide training program for them on equipment reliability, availability, maintainability, and safety. I conducted training workshops at most of their worldwide plant locations. This included the US, China, Japan, South Korea, Singapore, Taiwan, France, and Germany. The training was for all levels of managers and key engineers. However, this relationship did not last more than two years. The high-tech industry had a further decline. No one was spending any money on quality and reliability. Once I finished training key personnel, the training program was put on hold and was eventually suspended. I did a few auditing jobs and some volunteer ISO audits to maintain my RAB certification. But eventually, all the jobs in my field of interest died out. And I was getting comfortable with my new lifestyle of doing nothing.

B. Property Management

I was getting comfortable with my new lifestyle after the high-tech industry declined further, and I was not getting any consulting jobs. The situation suddenly changed in April 2012, when Neel's friend and business partner, David Russell (a chiropractor), got convicted of sexual charges and was sentenced to twenty-three years in jail. David and Neel owned a jointly developed, fourteen thousand-square-foot professional center in McKinney, Texas. Once David got incarcerated, Neel had to decide whether to: (i) let the mortgage lender take over the ownership and lose all the invested capital and capital appreciation, amounting to more than 1.5 million dollars, or (ii) take over 100-percent ownership and have me manage the property. Since I had some experience with real estate, Neel asked me whether I would be willing to take on ownership and management responsibilities. I could not help but jump in. I had to. I thought it was a call for my fatherly duty to help my kids in a tough time. This was the beginning of becoming a property manager and acting landlord.

When I took over the responsibility, the property had only one tenant, and the rest of the property was an empty shell. I got three new tenants, got the interior constructed for them, and made it fully leased. Once it got to that point, Neel and I decided to construct the second phase of the property, consisting of seven thousand square feet of leasable space. I got architectural plans developed, selected a contractor, and started construction. I supervised the construction with help from a construction engineer friend, Mr. Sharad Sevak. More than half of the second-phase space was preleased before the shell was completed. Eventually, all the shell space was leased and both buildings became 100-percent occupied.

Since I was living in Plano, more than twenty miles from the property, this responsibility was more than a full-time job. I had to deal with day-to-day operational issues, tenants' requests, property repairs and maintenance, rent collections, bill payments, minor financial decisions, accounting of expenses that were paid by the tenants, rent collections and deposits, relationships with tenants, cash flow accounting, interfacing with Neel's CPA, real estate taxes, liability insurance, service supplier management, dealing with real estate leasing brokers and keeping the property leased, and lots more. Later, I hired a part-time assistant property manager, Jan Elwell, to help me with the day-to-day operational issues. However, that did not reduce my workload significantly.

Fortunately, I was able to keep the property in well-maintained condition, fully leased, generating sizable income, and appreciating in value. This work gave me the joy of being useful to my son. It kept me occupied, sharp, and healthy.

7.7 PUTTING ROOT DEEPER IN THE LIVING DOMAIN OF THE TRANSPLANTED LAND

The above chapters 7.1 through 7.6 describe how I put my roots deeper and thrive in the business domain of the transplanted land. Very little has been said about putting my root deeper in the living domain of residential neighborhoods of the transplanted land.

Before coming to America, I lived in either my parents' home or a school dormitory in India. I did not know anything about living differently, particularly in a different county. I had many things to learn to live in the transplanted land.

A. Initial Exposure to Living in The Transplanted Land – Apartment Near IIT

As mentioned in chapter 5.1, my friend Vallabh Patel, Harish Patel, and I looked for an apartment in the area within walking distance from the IIT Campus. We rented a three-bedroom apartment above an old, rundown real estate office at 3038 Wentworth Ave, Chicago, IL 60616. It was located next to a dry-cleaning plant, in a run-down and intimidating area, right above a busy street, and next to a noisy Interstate 94. but it was within walking distance of the campus, a large grocery store, and a coin-operated Laundry. When we moved in, the landlady helped us to get our apartment furnished. To us, everything looked excellent. After we three settled down, the other three IIT students from India moved with us. Now we were six living in the three-bedroom apartment. This apartment living was the first experience for all of us to live in places other than either our parents' home or school dormitory. None of us knew how to operate kitchen gadgets, cook, clean dishes, pots, and pans, wash cloth, or shop for groceries and other necessities.

Necessities are the mother of invention; we quickly learned all the household chores. There were no Indian grocery stores in the Chicago area at that time. We figured out substitutes for our favorite Indian dishes. For breakfast, we ate toast, jam/jelly. Milk, juice cereal; for lunch we ate grilled cheese and veggie sandwiches; for dinner, we ate veggie soup, (made from green soup powder and frozen veggies), rice, and toast; and for snacks, we ate cookies and ice cream.

Once we mastered the day-to-day basic dishes, we explored making popular Indian dishes, on weekends, like roti, puri(fried roti), bhajia (fried veggie dumplings), ladoo (sweet ball), and fruit salad. Once our Indian friends, living in the dorms, found out that we can cook some Indian dishes, they bag to have the taste of Indian food. This led to our apartment becoming a weekend Indian feast center.

We were extremely busy with our studies and not much time was available for other things. By the time we completed one year of study, we all became knowledgeable about the daily tasks of an apartment living in the transplanted land.

Once I completed my coursework at IIT and got a job in north Chicago, I had to move near my job. A friend of mine was looking for a roommate for his apartment in north Chicago. I decided to move there as described in the next section.

B. North Chicago Apartment - 927 W Belle Plaine Ave Chicago, IL 60613

This apartment was on a bus route to my work. Since I didn't have a car then, this apartment was convenient to commute to work. It had one bedroom, a living room, a dining room, a bathroom, and a kitchen. It was in a nice, newer, and quiet area. The property owner kept it well-maintained.

My living style in this apartment was not much different than what I used at the previous apartment. The only difference was that we were two men living instead of six at the previous place. Because of that, I have to stay alone while my partner is working overtime or out with his girlfriends.

I lived in this apartment for less than seven months while completing my thesis and looking for a better job. Three good things happened while I was living in this apartment (i) learned to drive, (ii) got a life partner, and (iii) got a mechanical engineering job of my preference, with a reputable corporation, the Foster Wheeler Corporation, in Livingston, New Jersey.

Once I accepted the job at Foster Wheeler, I moved to Ivy Hill Park Apartments in Newark, NJ as described in the next section.

C. Ivy Hill Park Apartment – 65 Manor Dr. Apt. 14G, Newark, NJ 07106

The Ivy Hill Park Apartments complex is a multi-story, multi-building, and largest Apartment complex in New Jersey. For us, its location was convenient for commuting to Ney York City and my workplace. Besides, a grocery store, drug store, laundry, cleaner, bank, and public park with kids' play area were within walking distance. A few Indian families, including our close friend Kumar Kalola (see chapter 9.5), were already living there. Our apartment was on the 14th Floor with a panoramic view of New York City. It had one Bedroom, one Bathroom, a Livingroom Dining room combo, and a kitchen. The total living space was 550 sq. Ft.

I rented and furnished this apartment before Manju's arrival. We had our wedding in the basement party room of the apartment complex. When we moved in, many Indian families were living in the complex. Some of them became good friends. We all used to get together for Weekend card games and picnics at nearby parks Bear Mountain Park, NY, Longwood Gardens Philadelphia, Cherry Blossom Festivals in Washington, DC, Watkins Glens and Finger Lakes State Parks, beach and boardwalk at Atlantic City, NJ, and many more.

There wasn't any Indian grocery store in the area. We used to buy some Indian spices from a mid-eastern store in Manhattan and China Town. This forced us to discover substitute spices, available in the local grocery stores.

While we were living in this apartment, we had many friends and family visit us. Every visitor wanted to see New York City's top attractions like Time Square, United Nations Plaza, Empire State Building, Ellis Island/ Statue of Liberty, Rockefeller Plaza, and Radio City Music Hall. We took them around and became tour guides for them.

There were too many adults living there but very few children. They looked remarkably busy with their life. As a result, we didn't make any non-Indian friends at this apartment. However, we learned to survive in the transplanted land.

This apartment living gave us many lasting memories like our wedding, Neha's birth, baby Neha, and her first birthday party, and my going to evening school.

When Neha was a year and a half and we were expecting Neel, our close friend, Kumar Kalola moved to a Garden Apartment in Parsippany, NJ. We followed them.

D. Garden Apartment Living – 71 Camelot Rd Parsippany, NJ 07054

Living in a garden apartment was different that living in a High-Rise apartment. The apartment was roomy. It had more open space around the apartment, fewer tenants, and more friendly neighbors,

Our complex had only 50 families, many of them with little children, the same age as Neha and Neel. We made several non-Indian friends at this complex.

The main assess road had slight slop. Neel used to love going downhill on a scooter in summer and snow sledding in the winter. He also used to love the friendly Garbage Truck drivers.

This apartment living also gave us many lasting memories like Neel's birth, Neha starting school in kindergarten, my completing PhD degree requirements, and getting a good job with Xerox Corporation. This forced us to move to a Garden Apartment in Rochester, NY.

E. Garden Apartment Living – 345 West Squire Drive #2 Rochester, NY 14623

This garden apartment had almost the same features that we had in Parsippany NJ. Except, this complex was much bigger with more amenities. It had a clubhouse, tennis courts, and Swimming Pool.

We made many Indian and non-Indian friends during our short stay in Rochester. Since Rochester is within driving distance of Niagara Falls, we had a constant flow of friends and family visiting Niagara Falls.

While we were in Rochester, Neel started kindergarten Both Neha and Neel learned to swim.

One of the lasting memories of Rochester living is Sunday morning walking to the Dunkin Donut store to get donuts and a Sunday newspaper.

We lived in Rochester, NY for 18 months before I was transferred to Dallas TX.

F First House - Teakwood Lane, Plano, TX 75075

Since this was our first house, we didn't know much about the house's interior layout, construction material, location, conveniences, closeness to schools, and other local amenities. This house was purchased during a short trip for "house hunting" without thinking about the above items.

It had 4 Bedrooms, a Breakfast nook, a dining room, a living room, a covered patio, a two-car garage with a back entrance from an alley, and small back and front yards. It was in the middle of a long street.

After living four years in this house, we found out it had more things that we didn't like about it than the things we like about it. This inspired us to look for another home in the neighborhood.

G. Bigger/Better/ Home - 2605 Graphic Place, Plano, TX 75075

This house was, in a newly developed area, just three miles from the previous home. When we bought it, it was under construction. We had a chance to pick up interior finishing. We have been residing in this house since 1979 and it is our current residence. It has 4 Bedrooms, a Game Room, a Breakfast nook, a dining room, a living room, a large entrance area, two patios, two car side garage with a J Form driveway that can accommodate up to 12 cars, a large backyard adjoining a creek, a balcony overlooking backyard and creak, and is located on a small no-through traffic street. The interior layout is designed so that no cutting-through is required to go to any room.

This house is located within walking distance of (i) an elementary school, (ii) a high school, and (iii) a City Park with a walking trail. The Middle school, department stores, grocery stores, drug stores, cleaners, barbers, gas stations, post office, public library, city recreation center, doctors, dentists, a general and a specialty hospital, restaurants, and quick food pickup outlets are within a few minutes' drive.

After we moved into this house, many Indian friends moved into the neighborhood. It took little time to make many Indian friends. The residents living in the neighborhood were open-minded and friendly. We made many non-Indian neighbors our friends. Our both side next-door neighbors are very friendly and caring. They keep an eye on and take care of our house while we are out of town for a longer period. We do the same thing for them. Our Northside neighbor, Rich Hill, keeps dogs who keep eyes on the strangers walking in our driveway and yards.

While living in this house, we sponsored several family members and friends for permanent residency (Green Card). When they first arrived in America, this house gave initial temporary shelter to whoever moved into the Dallas area.

During more than forty years of living in this house, many long-lasting memories were created. To mention a few, raised Neha and Neel from elementary school thru their graduation from medical school; celebrated birthdays, anniversaries, graduations, mothers' and fathers' days, Christmas and Thanksgiving Holidays, Texas-OU Football games, Neel's wedding, and grandchildren visits.

While living in this house we continued learning the better ways of living in the transplanted land. At the same time, we matured and transformed a lot, which helped us put our roots deeper and thrive in the transplanted land. Now, at the tail end of the evolution process, we are an integral, distinguishable, and productive part of the transplanted land's living domain.

8

SPARE- AND LEISURE-
TIME ENDEAVORS

America offered me many opportunities to advance, grow, and blossom. While working for my employers as an engineer, as described in the previous chapters, and raising two kids, I attempted the following endeavors in my spare and leisure time. All endeavors gave me many challenges and learning opportunities. They helped me to be productive and creative in the transplanted land.

8.1 SELF-DEVELOPMENT

A. Enhancing Skills

One of the most valuable things I did in my spare time was to get a doctorate degree (PhD), as described in detail in chapter 7.2. Four things that helped me to achieve this goal were: (i) educational benefits available to employees of the Foster Wheeler Corporation; (ii) encouraging and supportive immediate supervisors and coworkers; (iii) a small family and young children; and (iv) a supportive life partner, Manju, who was not working and could take responsibility of raising our children.

Getting the doctorate degree put me in a special class of people in the world. I am thankful to the Foster Wheeler Corporation and my coworkers there, to New York University, and to Manju for this achievement.

While working at the Xerox Corporation and Texas Instruments, I learned more about the reliability engineering discipline by taking several short courses, studying (self-study), and attending symposiums. This gave me a total picture of the reliability discipline for any product life cycle phase which includes: (i) developing reliability goals/requirements, (ii) design in reliability, (iii) build in reliability, (iv) test for reliability, and (v) manage reliability improvement/growth for the units in operation at the customers' places.

I learned one more discipline while working for the Xerox Corporation. That was basic accounting. I took a course on accounting for managers, which was a remarkably high-level and highly concentrated course. It taught me the basics of accounting and how to read the financials of any organization.

Later, I used this basic accounting knowledge to learn QuickBooks accounting software. I used QuickBooks to manage Neha and Neel's account books, our family's limited partnerships account, and my personal finances.

This basic accounting knowledge also helped me to do volunteer work for the AARP Foundation Tax-Aide program, as described in chapter 11.1.

B. Yoga Classes

Learning yoga methodically was the second most valuable thing I did in my spare time.

I'd had some exposure to yoga when I was in school and college in India. During this period, I'd heard a lot about yoga practice and its benefits. But I never took a serious interest in joining any formal classes. However, I did do a few asanas, (yoga poses), like standing on my head and doing eye exercises. This did not take me anywhere.

Late in 2007, one of our friends (Sarita Gaitonde), a fellow trustee of the DFW Hindu Temple Society, told me about her plan to go to India and take yoga training under a very well-known yoga guru (teacher) for one year, and then she was planning to teach yoga classes at the temple when she returned. I promised her that I would be the first one in her class. She attended yoga training and got a certificate to teach yoga. When she returned from yoga training, she started her first yoga class at the DFW Hindu Temple, in January 2009. Manju and I both signed up for the class, which was scheduled for Sundays from 8:00 to 10:00 a.m. We continued with the classes for seven years.

Our yoga learning started with chanting *ohm* properly, using basic breathing techniques, doing simple asanas, attention-based concentration, calming down the mind, etc. As we advanced, we learned complex asanas, Kapalbhati and pranayama (breathing exercises), Surya Namaskar (sun salutation), body stretches, body stability, remaining in a thoughtless condition, sitting in one position without moving, beginning the meditative state, and many more.

Sarita's teaching style was very methodical and systematic. She broke down every asana into small steps and made sure that every student did it properly. She explained the physiological benefits of every asana. As a result, her teaching methodology was the most effective to teach us yoga asanas.

Manju and I both became staunch believers in yoga and benefited tremendously from the classes. We both owe a lot to Sarita for making a big change in our lives.

Once I retired, I continued, for the rest of my life, practicing yoga every day in the morning for about an hour.

8.2 STOCK MARKET INVESTMENTS

I did not know anything about the stock market until 1969. When our closest friend, Kumar Kalola, got his stockbroker's license and joined a small brokerage firm, he introduced me to the basic concept of investing in the stock market. He advised me to buy stocks of some new and growing companies. I made a small investment in the five companies.

Two companies' stocks gained quite a bit. I cashed out the profit and reinvested it in other stocks. Suddenly, the brokerage firm went under, and our stockholdings were locked up in the court battle. Since the broker was a market maker for these stocks, most of them became worthless. Our friend was devastated by the stockbroker's bankruptcy. He was sorry about getting all his friends stuck with losses. He left the stock trading job and went back to an engineering job. He stopped talking about stocks. So did I. This was my first lesson on stock investment, at the cost of a small capital loss. However, I did receive worthless stock certificates in exchange.

When I started working for the Xerox Corporation, I had the option to invest my profit-sharing amount in the retirement fund or take cash out. Since I did not need any cash, I started investing in the retirement fund, which was managed by the Xerox Corporation. At that time, Xerox was a very profitable company, and I used to get up to 20 percent of my salary in profit sharing. I invested all of it in the retirement fund. I had no knowledge of the investments in the retirement fund. But it was growing every year.

In 1980, our seven Indian friends, who were living in the Dallas-Fort Worth metroplex area, decided to start an investment club. I joined the club too. I learned a lot about stock market investing from this association with the investment club, including how to evaluate the desirability of a stock for investment. The stock buy/sell decisions were made after discussion and input from all the members. This process resulted in a better decision on stock selection. The club got a better-than-average return on the investment. I also used this knowledge for managing my personal portfolio. When two leading members moved from the Dallas-Fort Worth area, the club was dissolved. I was on my own, investing my savings in stocks.

Since I had learned my lesson of selecting a stockbroker, this time, I selected a top-notch stock brokerage firm, Merrill Lynch, for my personal portfolio. They provided an excellent knowledge base and stock analysis to manage my portfolio.

When I left Xerox, my retirement fund portfolio grew to a sizable amount. After I left Xerox, I had to roll over my retirement fund within one year to an individual retirement account (IRA) with a custodian of my choice. I selected Merrill Lynch and rolled over the fund to my IRA account with them. This rolled over and added one more stock brokerage account that I had to manage.

Later, I added brokerage accounts for Neel and Neha; our family's limited partnership; Manju, Neel and Neha's IRAs; Neha's 401(k); and my, Manju, and Neha's Roth IRAs.

When the total value of all the investment assets passed the one-million mark, I became a member of the Merrill Lynch Private Client Group, a preferred Merrill Lynch customer with many perks.

After 2000, the stockbroker business started changing. Cheaper and more efficient online brokers came into existence. Since Merrill Lynch was the top-notch broker in the arena and did not have online trading (at that time), their commission rates were extremely high. After studying several online brokers' performances, costs, and ratings, I selected Fidelity Investments for my stock market investing needs. Slowly, I transferred all the portfolios that I was managing to Fidelity. Eventually, I managed fifteen family accounts with combined assets of over several million dollars. In addition, I was partially responsible for managing the Gita Investment Club's portfolio (see chapter 12.4 on the Gita Investment Club).

In the long run, the stock market investment paid back handsomely. However, there were several incidents of market crashes. I had to live through those crashes and stay invested. Eventually, the market came back and continued growing.

8.3 Real Estate Investments

A. Apartment Building

In the late 1970s, while working at the Xerox Corporation, ten Indian Xerox employees invested in a fifty-unit apartment building in White Settlement, Texas, a suburb of Fort Worth. It was managed by Daulat Agrawal, one of the partners and a residential property manager. This was my first experience with real estate investment. It turned out to be an excellent investment. It had good cash flow and value appreciation. We bought it at the perfect time, when the real estate prices in the Dallas-Fort Worth area were not appreciated yet. In a few years, the occupancy rate, rent, and market value all went up significantly. All the partners were happy and looking to invest more in such apartment buildings in the Dallas-Fort Worth area. We could not buy any more, because none of them came close to this one in financial performance. When some partners started moving out of the area, the apartment building was sold at a good profit.

B. Mini Warehouses

This investment was another successful real estate investment. My coworker at the Xerox Corporation, Mr. Gilbert Castro, became a close friend (see details in chapter 9.5). He invited me to participate in his mini-warehouse project. He had his house on fifty acres of land on State Highway 407 in Lewisville, Texas. There were no mini warehouses in the vicinity. He carved out a forty-acre piece of land from his fifty acres and rezoned it for mini warehouses. We created the Gilval Partnership. Gilbert owned 75 percent, and I owned 25 percent of the partnership. We became general contractors and built the first phase of fifty units with our own capital money. All the units were rented even before we completed the construction. This encouraged us to build more units, and financing became easy. We started building and renting units. Eventually, we had five hundred units of various sizes. We named it Action Storage. It continuously remained 95 percent rented. Initially, Gilbert and his wife, Charlotte, managed the rental operations. Later, we constructed a two-bedroom apartment and a rental office at the entrance. We hired one couple to manage the renting operations. The couple lived in the apartment/office unit.

This project had a considerable positive cash flow. Gil and Charlotte used this financial capacity for constructing a big lakefront home in Little Elm, Texas. Charlotte had a very high-level job in a bank with a good salary. Everything was cruising great. Suddenly, Charlotte lost her job. For Gil, the cash flow from the mini warehouses was not enough to make the mortgage payments on the big house. He requested me to sell the mini warehouses. He also sold the new house and moved to a smaller house. We made a good profit when we sold the mini warehouses. I wished that, at the time, I'd had the capital to buy Gilbert's partnership and continue ownership of the mini warehouses.

This mini-warehouse project was a shining example of a business partnership based on friendship, trust, and mutual respect. We had a perfect combination of skills. Gil loved to get his hands dirty and work on any construction/maintenance issues. I was good at financing, accounting, income taxes, bookkeeping, computer work, and number crunching. During the partnership, we did not have a single controversy. We remained friends until his untimely death.

C. Land

When Gilbert Castro moved to his lakefront home in Little Elm, there were one hundred acres of a piece of land adjoining his property, which was for sale with no down payment. We grabbed it and started paying the monthly installment from the mini warehouses' positive cash flow. When Gilbert got in a financial bind and we sold the mini warehouses, we had no way to pay the monthly installments for the land we had purchased. At that time, I was laid off from Xerox and was struggling to pay for both kids' college educations. We decided to let the land go back to the original owner, after paying installments for five years. Again, I wished that I'd had the income at that time to pay for the monthly installments. This land investment could have been very profitable.

D. Single-Family Homes

When I was working for Xerox, one of my colleagues owned several single-family homes for rental purposes and used to talk about them a lot. I decided to try out being a landlord. We bought our first rental home in East Plano. We managed the rental operations and the property maintenance tasks. Our first tenant was very rough and damaged the home, so it required lots of maintenance. Once he moved out, we were lucky to get a mature and gentle couple with a small child. They stayed in the house for a long time. When they moved out, we sold the house with a sizable profit.

When I was a managing partner of the Century 21 office, our office bought several single-family homes at bargain prices and kept them for rental income purposes. When our partnership fell apart and we had to kick out our dishonest partner, the office owned eight homes. I received three homes in my share of the office assets. I kept them for a while. When managing and maintenance became difficult, I sold them all and got out of the landlord business.

8.4 SMALL BUSINESSES

A. Indian Grocery Store

This was a joint venture with Jayant Amin. He had a friend in Houston, Texas, who owned a thriving Indian grocery store there. We were shown its operation, and it looked very promising. So we decided to jump into the business and bought a running Indian grocery store, called Asia Import, in Dallas. Since Manju had lots of experience with retail business operations with Target stores, she took responsibility for the store's operations. I helped her to manage the financial bookkeeping and general maintenance. Later, Jayant Amin dropped out as a partner, and we added Jaysurya and Sharda as partners.

After three years of successful operation, the circumstances of the store ownership changed in three ways: (i) a large Indian grocery store opened nearby, which made the business operations competitive; (ii) the store lease was expiring, and the landlord almost doubled the rent to renew the lease; and (iii) we had the added responsibility of settling down my side of the family, who had immigrated to America. When we calculated the financial and family obligations for the changing circumstances, we realized that the return on our investment and time would be minimal. We decided to close the store and sell off the equipment and inventory.

For Manju, the store ownership and operations were very time-consuming. It was extremely hard on her, and on all of us.

B. Import Business

This was a joint venture with Kush Lakdawala, a good neighbor and a fellow Xerox employee. We both had relatives in Mumbai, and they encouraged us to start an import business in Dallas. Our relatives assured us that they would help us find the merchandise suppliers and arrange their shipment. With this in mind, we started the India Trade Center to import and sell merchandise to chain stores or individual store buyers. Initially, we concentrated on ladies' tops, maxi skirts, and sandals. We acquired merchandise samples for the merchandise that we were going to sell. To reach out to the buyers, we rented a showroom at the Dallas Market Center during their spring and fall fashion shows. We also went door to door vising buyers. We had some success in getting a few orders. When we ordered the merchandise from our suppliers, we started experiencing the suppliers' problems. They wanted cash payments before shipping the merchandise, they were missing the delivery date, and the quality of the merchandise was much inferior to the samples we had received from them. Because of these issues, we could not ship the merchandise to our customers on time and the quality of the merchandise was not what they'd expected from us. As a result, we got stuck with poor-quality merchandise that we had to sell at a fire sale at the flea market. After these initial experiences, we concluded that the import business was not our cup of tea. We discontinued the business.

C. Car Wash

When I was managing the Century 21 Office, our office got an opportunity to buy a running coin-operated car wash, with no down payment, and just take over the note payment responsibility. When our partnership fell apart and we kicked out our dishonest partner, the office owned the car wash. We kept it for a while and concluded that day-to-day management tasks such as collecting coins, refilling soap dispensers, repairing damaged spray wands, cleaning the area, etc. required lots of time and energy. We hired a manager to help us. Then came a breaking point when some crook figured out how to fool the coin-changer machine with phony dollar bills. We started getting hundreds of phony bills a day. After this unsolvable problem, we sold it and got out of the car wash business.

D. Lesson Instilling Failed Undertakings

In the early 1980s, I was very eager to get into some business. I trusted tempting advertisements in the local newspaper and sweet-talking scam artists. I made two sizable investments in such undertakings without thoroughly investigating their backgrounds. Once the money was paid, it turned out to be bogus. I paid a high price to learn my lesson: *never give money to any sweet-talking strangers.*

8.5 WORLDWIDE TRAVEL

While Neha and Neel were growing up, we traveled quite a bit within America visiting attractions for kids (such as Disneyland, Knott's Berry Farm, beaches, etc.) and famous landmarks of America (such as Niagara Falls; upstate New York; the Statue of Liberty; and Washington, DC landmarks). During our trips to India, we also visited a few countries on the way to India. The bulk of my worldwide travel occurred after I joined Texas Instruments. Since TI had branches in Europe and Asia, visiting those countries was part of my work. Whenever I had to travel solo, not as a member of a group, I took Manju with me. Jointly, we traveled to several countries in Europe and Asia. After Manju and I retired, we picked up the pace for worldwide traveling. Fortunately, we had a group of friends in the Dallas area who were in a similar situation; they were also physically active and interested in exploring the world. That created a cohesive group of friends, and we started planning land tours and cruises around the world. Manju and I joined most of the land tours and cruises. This enlarged our list of countries we'd traveled to. We were fortunate to travel to the following countries, most of them for pleasure, but some for both pleasure and business.

North American Countries

- Canada
- Mexico
- Panama
- Costa Rica
- Colombia
- Guatemala
- Belize
- Honduras
- Dominican Republic

European Countries

- United Kingdom
- Germany
- France
- Italy
- Sweden
- Spain
- Portugal
- Greece

Asian Countries

- Japan
- China
- South Korea
- Malaysia

- Thailand
- Cambodia
- Myanmar
- Singapore
- Hong Kong
- Taiwan
- Bali, Indonesia

Caribbean Islands

- Turks and Caicos
- Antigua
- Dominica
- St. Kitts
- St. Lucia
- St. Thomas
- St. John
- Cozumel

Other Countries

- Egypt
- Australia
- New Zealand

Every country we visited had its unique social and political cultures. Worldwide travel improved our perception and tolerance level of humanity. Also, we had opportunities to see the wonders of Mother Earth.

After all the worldwide travel, we concluded that no country on Earth is better than America for living.

9

ENABLERS

I was so fortunate to have numerous enablers in my life who have helped to shape my outlook, character, and personality to fit the cultured and modern society, to get an education, and eventually to get transplanted in America.

9.1 CARING UNCLES AND AUNTS

I had five uncles and two aunts on my father's side, and four uncles and four aunts on my mother's side. I had known all of them but was not close to all of them. Among all the uncles and aunts, I had close relationships with the following two uncles and one aunt. They cared for my well-being and helped me to achieve my life goals.

A. Uncle: Jasmat (Jasmat Kaka: 1915–1968)

My relationship with Uncle Jasmat was an incredibly unique uncle-nephew relationship.

He was the youngest and richest uncle on my father's side. When my grandfather died, he was only three years old. My grandmother and my father raised him. He was the first one to complete high school in the Dhudshia family.

Figure 9.1: Uncle Jasmat.

At that time, high school graduates were rare in our area. After high school graduation, he got a good job in government. When he participated in the Free India movement rally, he was fired from the government job. After that, he started his own business and became a successful businessman in tobacco products manufacturing and distributing.

He lived in Vanthali, only three miles from our hometown of Shapur. When I was young, I used to admire his high-class lifestyle, nice house with modern amenities, entertainment equipment like a gramophone, and modern toys for his kids. He was kind to all his nephews and nieces. When he visited us in Shapur, he used to bring sweets for us kids and his gramophone to entertain all of us. On every New Year's Day, I used to go to see him and get his New Year's blessings. He used to give us blessings and money.

Until I became a senior in high school, I did not have any special relationship with him. When I was in my final year of high school, he started taking a very keen interest in me and my career plans. I was the second person in the Dhudshia family to graduate from high school (after him). He was proud of my achievement (my being the first one to go to college in the Dhudshia family) and supportive of my continuing further education and going to college. When I was in junior college in Junagadh and engineering college in Morbi, he used to visit me in my hostel (dormitory) and would encourage me to continue my education. Since I was always at the top of the class, he was proud of my educational success.

During the summer vacation of 1962, I told my parents, my brother, Devraj, and him about my plans to go to America for further study. He was thrilled and supportive of my plan. He also assured me that he would do anything within his ability to make my plans materialize. With his assurance and blessings, I started activities to go to America for further study.

When I started preparing for further study in America, he and I became even closer. Until that time, I had not needed any financial help from anyone. He lent me five thousand rupees and promised to help me to raise funds for my study in America. He took a very keen interest in my plans and preparations. He also advised me about getting married. He was taking pride as an uncle of an American-going student.

Since I was the first one to graduate from college, he started getting my advice for his kids about getting a college education. I helped his son Mohan and his daughter Mukta to enroll in college, and I provided guidance for them to succeed in college. They both became my closest cousins among all the cousins I have.

When I was leaving India for the first time, he took time out of his business and came with me to Mumbai to bid me farewell. I spent my last day before leaving India with him and my brother Devraj in Mumbai. On the day of my departure, I saw pride and sorrow on his face. I took his blessings before going onto the ship. I still remember his face as he waved goodbye at the port when the ship started leaving. At that time, I did not know that was the last time I would see his face.

Lots of credit goes to him and my cousin-sister Labhuben (his daughter) for my marrying Manju. They both recommended that I should marry Manju and were happy that I did, as described earlier in chapter 6.

He used to write very emotional and touching letters to me when I was settling down in America. Those letters provided the emotional support I needed to establish roots in the transplanted land.

His love, advice, pride, and encouragement meant a lot to me in my life. I consider myself a lucky nephew to have had such an uncle.

A few years after I came to America, he developed throat cancer. I offered my help for him to come to America and have an operation. He did not take it. He got it operated in India. However, the cancer came back with vengeance, and he died, after suffering a lot, in March 1968. I did not get a chance to see him when we went to India for the first time in April 1968.

B. Uncle: Vasharam (Vasharam Mama: 1920–2007)

He was my mother's youngest brother. He took care of my grandmother Moti. Since Grandmother was living with him, he always took care of us whenever we went to visit Grandma. Among all the maternal uncles, he was closest to me.

Figure 9.2: Uncle Vasharam.

He lived a basic, simple life in a small town called Dhandhusar. He was totally uneducated but was a very honest, hardworking, soft spoken, and loving person.

He was very street-smart and practical. With hard work on a small piece of land, he raised three boys and three girls. Two of his boys got some education and got out of poverty and farming. He used to wear chorano (white, narrow trousers), a regular shirt, and a white turban. He had a sweet, musical voice. He loved singing local folk songs. Since he had no education, he remembered all the songs. I had an opportunity to tape some of his songs for his memory.

Since I had a close relationship with him during my childhood, he took a very keen interest in my going to America. When I started raising funds for my study in America, I did not ask him for financial help. I thought he may not have the funds to lend me. But he surprised me. He came forward and told me that he would like to lend me five thousand rupees from his life savings, for my study in America. He was proud of my personal achievements. I was the only nephew, among all that he had, who graduated from college and went to America.

He used to keep a clipping from a local newspaper about my going to America, which he used to show to everyone with pride. He kept that clipping for a long, long time.

I was able to pay back his loan quickly and helped him in his old days, which he took very reluctantly. He believed that the maternal uncle should not take any money from his nephews.

I had the opportunity to visit him several times during my trips to India. Neha and Neel had an opportunity to meet him too. He used to own a manual rifle. Neel had a chance to fire it. He died in his eighties, due to old-age complications, a few months after I'd visited him in a hospital in Rajkot, India.

C. Aunt: Nandu (Nandu Masi: 1922–2007)

She was my mother's youngest sister. I have a fond memory of playing with her when I was young and used to visit my grandparents in Dhandhusar. She used to tease me for being from a bigger village and wearing different styles of clothing than those worn by the local boys. She was a very loving and cuddly aunt. She had a sweet and soothing voice. I loved listening to her talk and sing local folk songs. She was totally uneducated but was very honest and hardworking. After marriage, she moved to the town of Ajab and raised her family there. At a later age, she moved in with her oldest son, a bank officer, in Junagadh.

I had the opportunity to visit her several times during my trips to India. She died in her eighties, due to old-age complications, a year after I'd visited her in a hospital in Junagadh, India.

9.2 SUPPORTIVE SIBLINGS

A. Sister: Shanta (Shantaben: 1924–1995)

She was my eldest sister. She got married at an early age of five (the victim of child marriage) and went to her husband's place in Pipalia long before I started knowing her.

She was very pretty and slim, with a sweet voice. She was a loving and caring sister. When I was in second grade, my siblings and I stayed with her, as refugees, for about

Figure 9.3: Sister Shanta.

a year during the India-Pakistan division and migration from the Junagadh kingdom. She fulfilled all of our needs.

Like my mother, she was uneducated. Since her husband was mild-natured, she ran her household and managed the farms and the family. She worked extremely hard her entire life.

Since she had a big family of three boys and three girls, she never had enough money to live comfortably. Only one of her children got enough education to get out of poverty. I wanted her to come to America with her son Vasant (who received technical training in radio engineering), but she decided not to come. I helped her out during bad farming crop years. I also helped her sons to build a house and start a business. She died at the age of seventy-two, due to heart failure.

B. Sister: Jamuna (Jamunaben: 1928–2015)

She was my second eldest sister. I was her baby brother. She took care of me as a toddler when my mother was working. Because of our childhood bond, she became my favorite sister, and I developed a close relationship with her. Our close relationship continued in our adult lives.

Like my mother and other sisters, she was uneducated. She married a person in Shapur at an early age (a child marriage). Her first marriage did not work out due to her mother-in-law's problems. My father could not see her miserable situation, and he rescued her from the bad marriage.

Figure 9.4: Sister Jamuna.

She remarried to Velaji Panara, an elementary school teacher. Later, he had a small grocery store in Thaniyana. Sister Jamuna and her husband were very street-smart and farsighted people. They understood the value of educating their children. They used me as a role model for their children.

She had three boys and four girls. All her boys got a good education (one became a doctor, one a civil engineer, and one a business major). Not only that, but all her girls, except the oldest one, got a good education, too.

Two of her daughters also got a college education. I provided monetary and moral support for their education. Because of their education, all her children came out of poverty and farming.

I sponsored her to get permanent residency (a green card) in America. She could not handle the stress of the green card requirements and process. She let the opportunity go. Later, I had an opportunity to arrange the marriage of her eldest son Jaysukh (who was a doctor) to my close friend Vithal Patel's niece Tara (who had a green card). After their marriage, Jaysukh got his green card, came to America, completed the residency requirements, and received privileges to practice as a physician in America.

After Jaysukh and Tara settled down in America, he sponsored all his siblings and parents to get green cards. Finally, she, her husband, and all her children immigrated to America. They all settled in Charlotte, North Carolina, except Jaysukh, who settled in his practice in Tampa, Florida. Once she immigrated to America, I was in constant contact with her, either by phone or by visiting her. Among all my sisters, she was the luckiest one. In her old age, she enjoyed the luxury of a higher standard of living and had caring and loving relationships with her children and grandchildren. One of the things I always admired about her was her bonds with her daughters-in-law. Some lucky mother-in-law!

Her husband died in 2007, and she died on April 25, 2015. I happened to be at her deathbed when she passed away. I could not attend her funeral. However, I was able to attend after-death rituals.

C. Brother: Vithal (Vithalbhai: 1930–2005)

He was my eldest living brother when I was growing up. Since our age difference was so big, I never got to bond with him closely. However, he loved me and respected my growing up differently. Once he was living away from home, I used to spend a few days with him during summer vacations.

He was a smart student but did not continue his education after sixth grade. My father tried to send him to Africa to work with one of our relatives. He did not accept the opportunity. My parents bought a partnership (using my mother's savings) in a grocery store in Dhoraji and put him there to co-run the store. Another partner cheated on him and made a big loss. Within two years, he got disheartened and got out of the partnership with a big loss of the capital investment.

Figure 9.5: Brother Vithal.

Later, he got on-the-job training as a town clerk and got a government job. He worked the rest of his life as a town clerk for small village governments around Shapur. He also received a big chunk of farms and real estate from my parents. Some of the land he received from my parents was rezoned as a residential area. He received good money from the land sale and became very well-to-do. However, he never lived up to his financial condition. He lived a quite simple, basic life. He rarely spent any money on himself (not even on medical expenses). He rarely traveled outside the Saurashtra area.

He had two boys and three girls. He gave a good education to each of his children. Because of that, all of them are well-settled in India. He was very independent-minded and self-supporting. I encouraged him to launch a big family business with my financial support. He did not want that. He would rather go on his own. I also offered him financial help, but he did not take it.

He loaned me three thousand rupees when I came to America, which I paid back within two years. I offered to sponsor him and his children to receive green cards for America. He decided not to accept my offer.

He rarely went to see doctors, only whenever he was seriously ill. He had high blood pressure but never took any medication. Because of that, he got a stroke, and he became partially paralyzed at an early age. I made a special trip to see him in a paralyzed condition. He died on October 26, 2005, a few months after my visit.

D. Brother: Devraj (Devrajbhai: 1935–)

Figure 9.6: Brother Devraj.

I have spent more time with my brother Devraj than with any of my other siblings. We were close to each other. When I was a young boy, I used to follow him and his friends. He did not mind me hanging around them. He supported my going to school and not joining him on the farms. I respected, loved, and cared for him more than any other sibling. Not only that, but I have also financially helped him and his family more than I have for any other sibling.

He was a very smart student but never capitalized on his strength. He was a dedicated son. He always respected his parents. Just before I started college, he went to Kolhapur to venture into a new career with a relative who had a business there. He could not take the family separation and came back after a year. If he had succeeded there, our family would have changed a lot.

During the summer vacation of 1962, I told my parents, my uncle, and him about my plans to go to America for further study. He was thrilled with my plans and supported my goals. He also assured me that he would do anything within his ability to make my plans materialize. With his assurance and blessings, I started activities to go to America for further study. My parents and he were ready to sell our land to raise the needed funds. I told them not to do that. Instead, we sought funds from our relatives. He helped me to raise funds for my studies in America. He took a very keen interest in my plans and preparations. He also advised me about getting married. He was taking pride as a brother of an America-going student. He prepared a handwritten advisory memorandum book and gave it to me as a departing gift.

When I was leaving India for the first time, he came with me to Mumbai to bid me farewell. I spent my last day before leaving India with him and my uncle Jasmat in Mumbai. On the day of my departure, I saw pride and sorrow on his face. I took his blessings before going onto the ship. I still remember his face as he waved goodbye at the port when the ship started leaving.

He used to write very emotional and touching letters to me when I was settling down in America. Those letters provided the emotional support I needed to establish roots in the transplanted land.

His love, advice, pride, and encouragement meant a lot to me in my life. I consider myself lucky to have had such a supportive, caring, and loving brother.

Raising the standard of living for my parents and my brother Devraj's family was my top priority. During my early days in America, I sent him most of my savings. He and I jointly bought more land and cultivated the mango tree grove. We bought a partnership in a raw sugar factory and built new residential quarters. His family started enjoying an upper-middle-class lifestyle. With my monetary help and his hard work, his family's living standard came up very quickly. All his children got good educations and were well placed.

As detailed in chapter 11.2, when I became an American citizen, I applied for and got approval for immigration visas (green cards) for him and his family. When he received his green card and came to America, he lived with us for six months. I applied for an immigration visa for both of his sons, Raju and Anil. After their applications got approved, my brother decided to send only one son, Anil, to America.

Later, I renounced my ownership of our joint properties in Shapur by taking whatever money he offered and giving him full ownership.

Since I was unable to care for my parents' day-to-day living needs in India, he took responsibility with my monetary support. He was a dedicated son, and he took good care of our parents throughout their lives, with help from his wife, Mithibhabhi, and Shamjibhai.

9.3 OTHER SIBLINGS

Besides the above four supportive siblings, I have the following three siblings.

A. Brother: Viraji

He was my father's first child and the first boy in the Dhudshia family. I do not know much about him. The only thing I know is that he died in a drowning accident when he was four years old. Ever since my parents never allowed their kids near water and rivers. This was one of the reasons I never learned to swim.

B. Sister: Diwali (Diwaliben: 1937–2018)

Figure 9.7: Sister Diwali.

She was my elder sister and was close to my age. I lived with her more than any other sister. However, I never developed a close relationship with her. We used to have sibling rivalries and differences in our lifestyles. I was going to school, and she grew uneducated, helping my mother in the kitchen. We had no common interests in playing together. On the contrary, we used to have sibling fights often.

She married Chhaganlal Vachhani, a rich grocery store owner's eldest son, in a small town called Bhukhi. He was extremely hardworking and the key person to run his father's business. Her mother-in-law was an unlikable person. She could not tolerate her mother-in-law at all. She left her husband and in-laws, and her marriage was in trouble. However, a solution was worked out in which her husband got separated from his rich parents and the business. He and my sister started living independently.

In anger, her father-in-law gave her husband, Chhaganlal, a small piece of land and a small house to live in. He did not get a fair share of his father's big estate. As a result, they became poor and remained poor. They gave good education to their only son and some of their daughters. Their son never got out of his parents' shadows and remained a small farmer after receiving his master's degree. In 1978, I offered to sponsor her son to get permanent residency (a green card) in America. She and her son decided not to come to America. Later, she regretted her decision not to send her son to America. But it was too late. I gave her a large amount of money to build or buy a new house.

She developed osteoporosis in her early seventies. She died in 2018, at the age of eighty-one, due to complications from osteoporosis.

C. Sister: Anjani (1947–)

Figure 9.8: Sister Anjani.

She was my parents' youngest child. She had a twin sister who did not survive. Since she was the youngest, she got more attention from my parents. She survived a smallpox episode and a bite from a mad dog. When she was growing up, girls' educations were a key focus in the community. She was the only girl who got an education in our family.

After I came to America, she was enrolled in a boarding house in Rajkot, which she did not like. I insisted she remain in school. I provided financial support for her education. She graduated from the art college without the English language. She married Chimanlal Kasundra, a very mellow, tolerant, and accommodating electrical engineer. I paid all her wedding expenses. I tried to get Chimanlal admission into American universities but failed. When I became an American citizen, I sponsored them (Anjani, Chimanlal, and their sons Amul and Digant) to get green cards. When they arrived in America, I helped them to settle down in the Dallas area.

9.4 GENEROUS IN-LAWS

Figure 9.9: In-Laws.

My parents gave me life and supported me until I become a grown man. My in-laws gave me a life partner to live with for the rest of my adult life. I blossomed, in the transplanted land with support from my life partner. Lots of credit goes to my in-laws for raising a well-rounded daughter and then giving me a compatible life partner. It is the most generous gift anyone can ever give!

A. Father-in-Law: Mohanlal G. Patel (1919–2014)

My father-in-law was born in a small village called Timbdi in Gujarat, India. He was the eldest among his siblings, with three brothers and five sisters. His father was a farmer and commodity trader. When my father-in-law was fifteen years old, his father lost lots of money in commodity trading and became depressed and withdrew from his family obligations. My father-in-law had to take over the family responsibility at the early age of fifteen. He quit school after high school and gave up his plan to become an engineer.

With borrowed funds, he moved to Mumbai and started a small grocery store. He worked very hard with honesty and fairness. He never took advantage of his customers. As a result, he became a very successful and popular local, small grocery store owner.

He was a visionary person. He did not get an opportunity for education. But he worked diligently to provide that opportunity to his siblings and children. As a result of his efforts, two of his brothers became doctors, one brother became a postmaster, each of the sisters got at least a high school education, and all his children got college educations.

Besides working very hard for his business and family, he supported the Mumbai-area Kadwa Patidar community organization's finance management.

When Manju became an American citizen in 1974, she sponsored all her siblings to get American residency (green cards). Once all of Manju's siblings came to America and had settled down in their chosen professions, they sponsored their parents to get American residency (green cards).

After getting their green cards, he and my mother-in-law shuttled back and forth between America and India. At an advanced age, when he had a minor stroke, he made America their permanent place of residence. Later, they sold off their residence in Mumbai, India, and stayed in America for the rest of their lives.

Generally, he was in good health, even after the minor stroke. He lived a very regular life and continued exercising. But slowly, it deteriorated, and he passed away due to old-age complications at the advanced age of ninety-five.

B. Mother-In-Law: Vajkuvar M. Patel Ba (1923 – 2023)

My mother-in-law was born in a small village called Gingani in Gujarat, India. Her father was an accountant who worked in Africa, and her mother was living in Gingani, raising the family. When she was two years old, her mother took her to Africa to live with her father. Her mother did not like living in Africa, so both came back to India. She was raised by her mother while her father was still working in Africa. She was the middle child in a family of three boys and two girls. When she was growing up, girls' education was not popular. She quit school after third grade.

When she was around 5 years old, she married Mohanlal Patel, a child marriage. When she turned eighteen, she went to her in-law's place. During the early part of her married life, she worked on farms and later moved to Mumbai in 1945 with her husband and two-year-old eldest daughter, Manju. This was a big change in her lifestyle, moving from a small village to a big city. She quickly adopted a new lifestyle and became a skilled housewife and mother. Living among a smorgasbord of several cultures, she learned to live with them and cooked many varieties of dishes besides Gujarati dishes.

While raising her five kids, she developed hobbies in embroidery and beadwork. She made several very intricate pieces of her embroidery and beadwork. They are treasures for her kids and grandkids.

When she immigrated to America, she adapted to a combination of Indian and American lifestyles very quickly. She and my father-in-law were a great team to babysit their grandkids.

She is a very independent thinker. She lives in the present and enjoys every minute of it. She is loving, courteous, and practical. She never complains about any personal needs.

When she was eighty-one years old, she was diagnosed with a heart valve problem and clogged arteries. With Neha and Neel's advice, all her kids decided to go ahead with the risky heart valve replacement and bypass surgery. Her surgery was successful, and she became more energetic.

Regarding her health, she was a fighter. Up to the age of ninety-eight, she was mobile on her own. Later, she needed a little help to move around. She hanged onto her life in a reasonable condition and became the first in the family to reach one hundred years of age!

After living a happy, healthy, well-lived, and long life, she passed away on April 24, 2023.

9.5 ENRICHING FRIENDS

I was an ordinary farmer's son. My father and elder brothers had only elementary school educations, and my mother and elder sisters had no formal education. My family members had no idea how to shape my personality to fit the cultured and modern society. However, all of them were very supportive of me becoming cultured and modern. It took lots of help from my friends to shape my outlook, character, and personality.

I've made hundreds of friends during my lifetime, starting from elementary school and then through middle school, high school, junior college, engineering college, postgraduate education, working for employers, and getting involved with the surrounding community.

Each of them has enriched and shaped my life. I learned a little bit from every one of them at every stage of my life. When I reflect on my childhood, I feel lucky to have had such a large group of friends throughout my life. I feel like I was a clump of clay, and each friend gave a little shape, here and there, to the clump and made a gorgeous statue of me out of the clay clump. All of them created lots of good memories for me to cherish.

Several of my close coworkers and local friends could not believe my childhood status and how I had transformed from my childhood to my adult stage. I told them that I was lucky to have many enriching friends.

Out of all the friends I've made, the following come to the top of the list of those who have helped me the most to become who I am.

Figure 9.10: Vallabh Patel.

A. Dr. Vallabh T. Patel (Bhut), PhD

Our friendship started when I started seventh grade at the city middle school in Junagadh. We were in the same class. We both had similar family backgrounds. Just like me, he came from a small farming village and his parent were ordinary farmers. He was staying at the Patel Boarding House for his study in Junagadh. I was commuting by train. Since he started at the city middle school one year earlier than I did, he had already changed his outlook from a village boy to a city boy when I met him.

We had some natural affinity because of our similar family backgrounds and being Patel. We became friends very quickly. Once we became friends, he helped me to change my outlook from a village boy to a city boy.

He was an exceptionally bright student and captured top-of-class positions. I was also a bright student, just a notch behind him.

When we started Junagadh High School, he encouraged me to join the Patel Boarding House rather than commuting daily. I tried it, but I did not like the regimented living. I continued commuting by train for both of my high school years.

After high school graduation, he completed his undergraduate studies in mechanical engineering at Sardar Patel University in Vallabh Viyanagar. I completed my undergraduate studies in mechanical engineering at Gujarat University (Junagadh and Morbi). We remained close friends and stayed in constant contact during our undergraduate studies. During the final year of our undergraduate studies, we both decided to go to America for further study. We helped each other to get information and apply for admission to American universities. We both got admission to the Illinois Institute of Technology in Chicago, Illinois, and we decided to accept the admission. We helped each other to prepare for our journey to America, the unknown land of opportunities. We gave each other support and company during our journey to America, getting used to American life, and MSME study at IIT.

When we completed our MSME courses, he got a good engineering job at IBM in Poughkeepsie, New York, and he moved there. I could not find a good engineering job until I graduated. Once I graduated, I got a good engineering job at the Foster Wheeler Corporation in Livingston, New Jersey. We started living within driving distance of each other and continued seeing each other during the weekends. He played one of the main roles in my wedding.

Once I settled down in my married life and at my job, he encouraged me to continue for my PhD at New York University (NYU) at their campus in the Bronx. He'd already completed two years at NYU before I started.

Once I graduated from NYU, I got a better job at the Xerox Corporation in Rochester, New York, and I moved there. He took a teaching sabbatical and moved to South Carolina. Once we moved away from the New York and New Jersey areas, our contact became a little rusty. He later became a hotel/motel investor/operator, and I stayed in engineering. This took us farther away from each other. However, we created many sweet and unforgettable memories during our long friendship. I cannot thank him enough for his contribution to my outlook, character, and personality.

B. Velankar Family

Figure 9.11: Velankar family.

During my final year of high school, Mr. Velankar and his wife, Suman, moved to Shapur to manage Science Place, a Government of India project to spread use of basic science in the local population. I became a very close friend of the couple. He wanted young and enthusiastic volunteers for his project. For me, this was a great opportunity. I helped him to get familiar with the area and the local population.

I also helped him set up a basic science exhibition hall and accompanied him to show local people informative short movies about the use of basic science in day-to-day life. I also arranged for my father's help to spread basic science in the farming community.

Until I met the Velankars, I did not associate with any college-educated couple. Since they both were college graduates and broad-minded from cultured families, I learned a lot from both. Mainly, I learned social skills for communicating freely with upper-class, educated people and sophisticated ladies. They gave me an excellent opportunity to socialize with them in my hometown. Not only that, but Mr. Velankar gave me a rare chance to socialize with his younger sister Manda when she visited him during vacation after high school graduation.

They took a keen interest in my education and encouraged me to get a college education. They became my mentors. They also became family friends. My mother and father invited them for a pure Gujarati dinner. Our families went together on one day trip to the Somnath temple.

I continued my friendship with the Velankars while I was in college. I met them during my breaks. The Velankars and other local friends arranged a grand going-away party to celebrate my going to America.

I am very grateful to them for expanding my horizon and for providing guidance for me to succeed in my life.

C. Mathur Mori

Figure 9.12: Mathur Mori.

Our friendship started in June 1958, when I started my first year at Bahauddin College in Junagadh. My eldest brother, Vithal (who worked as a clerk in Mathur's town), found out that Mathur and I are third cousins. When I started college, my brother gave me heads-up to look for Mathur Mori in my class. Since it was a small student body and we were both living in the hostel (dorm), it did not take me long to find Mathur Mori.

Since we both had similar family backgrounds and were sons of ordinary, little-educated farmer families from a small village, we had a natural affinity to become friends.

We started liking each other. We dined together every day in the same mess, walked together to our classes, and took the same courses. This made our friendship flourish. Unfortunately, Mathur did not get admission to engineering college, and I did. We took separate paths for further study. However, we remained in close contact during our studies. He did his bachelor's and master's degrees in physics and started teaching physics at a local college. I completed a bachelor's degree in engineering and came to America. We continued our close friendship. During my family's first visit to India, in 1968, we visited him and his family. During this visit, I encouraged him to come to America using the new visa policy for individuals with advanced degrees. He took advantage of the new visa policy and got a permanent visa (a green card) for America. He came to America, without his family, in October 1971, stayed with us for a few days, and then went to his cousin's place in Scranton, Pennsylvania. During the same time, we moved to Rochester, New York. He stayed in Scranton, Pennsylvania until his family—Vijuben, Shailesh, and Jay—arrived, and they moved to Hoboken, New Jersey. We continued our friendship and visited each other.

When we moved to the Dallas, Texas, area and settled down, Mathur completed a nuclear medicine course and was looking for a job. I suggested he look for a job in the Dallas area. He did, and he found a job of his liking, in the Dallas area, and moved there in 1976 with his family. We helped them to settle down in the area. Now that Mathur and his family were living close to us, our friendship got much stronger. Our kids were the same age. Our kids felt that they had found their cousins. Manju and I were happy to have Mathur, Vijuben, Shailesh, and Jay living close by. It was good to have a dependable and close friend living within twenty miles.

Slowly, he and his family got integrated into our circle of friends. We all, adults and kids, grew together. Our families participated in Gita Forum activities, such as garba, Diwali dinners, fundraising events, and summer campouts. Similarly, we also participated together in the DFW Hindu Temple Society activities. We helped each other during important events of our lives, such as birthday parties, graduation parties, weddings, and family deaths.

Our relationship is more than just as close friends. He is like a brother to me. I can depend on him for anything, at any time of the day or night. My kids also know about our close relationship. They know where to go for help when I am not available.

Mutual respect, honesty, and not expecting anything were key factors in our lifelong relationship.

D. Jaysukh Ranparia

Figure 9.13: Jaysukh Ranparia.

Our friendship began when I started my second year at the Lukhdhirji Engineering College. He was a good friend of Bhavanji Raiyani (details in the next section). I had a natural affinity with him because he was, just like me, well-organized and neat in day-to-day life, and meticulous in engineering drawings and workshop assignments. He became a member of our evening walks after dinner.

These walks were very enriching. We walked, talked, and argued about the current and future political and social situations. He and I did not like the quality and cost of the food served in the student hostel co-op mess (eating facility). Greedy, dishonest student managers ran it very poorly. The food bills were high, and the food quality was poor. We convinced the student hostel rector to give us the opportunity to manage the mess. We jointly managed the mess and turned the situation around with honesty, hard work, and skilled management. We provided excellent, quality food with more variety and at a lower cost. Not only that, but we were also able to install ceiling fans in the dining room and provided uniforms for the serving staff. We became very popular mess managers on campus. The engineering college's principal requested us to continue the mess management during our final year too. We did it only for the first semester. We wanted more study time during our final semester.

We continued our friendship and communication after I came to America. He got married and took a job in his in-law's construction company. Right after my marriage, his father-in-law developed throat cancer and came to New York for an operation. Manju and I helped him and his brother to facilitate their visit. They stayed with us, and we helped them to commute to and from the New York hospital during pre-op visits, hospital stays, and follow-up rehab visits. This help was sincerely appreciated by all his family members, and our friendship became strong.

He was not happy with his job in Mumbai. He wanted to immigrate to America. During our 1968 India visit, I encouraged him, just like I did to Mathur Mori, to come to America using the new visa policy for individuals with advanced degrees. He took advantage of the new visa policy and got a permanent visa (a green card) for America, using my sponsorship.

After he immigrated to America, he settled down in the Philadelphia, Pennsylvania, area and later moved to Charlotte, North Carolina. We continued meeting each other often. Later, he developed incurable diseases and died at an early age. We continued our contact with his wife, Puspaben.

E. Bhagvanji Raiyani

Figure 9.14: Bhagvanji Raiyani.

Our friendship began when I started at the Lukhdhirji Engineering College in Morbi. He and I had almost identical family backgrounds and junior college education. That made a natural fit for our friendship. He was in his second year of engineering college and was senior to me. That did not stop us from being friends. He and I liked to take walks after dinner, which brought us closer.

Once he graduated, he started working for a big construction company in Mumbai. He was an initiative-taker and an entrepreneurial-minded person. After working a couple of years for a construction company, he started his own construction company. The timing was perfect for him because there was a construction boom in Mumbai at that time. He became a successful builder in Mumbai.

Since he was a social reformer, he married a non-Patel lady. It was a very daring move for him. I did not even try it. His wife happened to be Manju's classmate.

We continued our friendship, even after I came to America. We stayed in constant contact and visited him during every visit to India. He visited us in America several times. We continued our long-distance friendship.

F. Kirit Shah

**Figure 9.15:
Kirit Shah.**

Our friendship also started at the Lukhdhirji Engineering College in Morbi. We had totally different family backgrounds. He was a son of a businessman from Mumbai. His family members were educated and cultured, and they lived in Mumbai, a big city. Despite these vast differences in our family backgrounds, we had a natural affinity and became close friends. He also used to join us for dinner and after-dinner walks and participated in interesting discussions. These meetings made us close friends.

While I was still in India, he invited me to his most elaborate wedding. His

**Figure 9.16:
Mahesh Dixit.**

wedding was the only friend's wedding I had attended in India. We continued our friendship after graduating from engineering college, and even after I came to America. We stayed in constant contact, and I visited him during every visit to India. He visited us in Plano, Texas. We continued our long-distance friendship.

G Mahesh Dixit

Our friendship also began at the Lukhdhirji Engineering College in Morbi. We had totally different family backgrounds. He was a son of the manager of a large city. All his family members were educated and cultured. They lived in a big city. Despite these vast differences, we had a natural affinity and became close friends. We stayed in the same hostel, and our rooms were in the same wing. During my final year, I had an opportunity to meet his family members, including his parents, three brothers, and two sisters. They all were respectful and affectionate. His younger sister Rajoo (see the following section) became a close friend after she immigrated to America.

After he graduated from engineering college, I helped him to come to America on a student visa.

He was a priest, and he performed our wedding ceremony using the Hindu wedding instruction guide. Later, he got his fiancée to come to America and got married to her, in a similar way to how Manju and I were married.

He worked in the New York and New Jersey areas and remained there. Once we moved away from that area, our contact became a little rusty.

H Kumar Kalola

Figure 9.17: Kumar Kalola.

He came to America three years before I did. Our families had similar backgrounds and lived in the same district. I knew about him before I came to America, and I started corresponding with him after I came to America. We may be fourth or fifth cousins. Once I got my job at Foster Wheeler, I rented an apartment in the same building where he was living. He and his wife, Vijuben, helped me a lot to get established in my new job and apartment. At that time, I did not have a car, and I depended on their help a lot. They had a large group of Indian friends who lived in the vicinity. Once Manju came, she also got integrated with their group.

He and his wife provided crucial support for our wedding. Since our parents and relatives could not come from India for our wedding, he became our guardian. In our wedding invitations, he was designated as the host of the event.

We lived in the same high-rise apartment complex for a while. We took many weekend visits together to nearby places. Eventually, we both moved to Parsippany in a garden apartment. We continued our friendship there, too.

I learned many social and living skills, including stock market investment, from him. We were so close that I could depend on him for help at any time of the day. After we moved out of the New Jersey area, we continued our friendship and contact. He and his wife were our important guests at my son Neel's wedding.

I. Rajoo Patel/Dixit

Figure 9.18: Rajoo Patel.

Rajoo is my friend Mahesh Dixit's younger sister. When I visited his home in 1963, I met all his family members, including her. She was very affectionate and treated me with respect, as she did to her elder brother, Mahesh Dixit. After she immigrated to America, started living with Mahesh Dixit in the Philadelphia area. At that time, we used to meet her often. Once she got married to Ramesh Patel, she changed her last name to Patel, and she moved with him to Poughkeepsie, New York. We stayed in contact continuously. I attended her daughter's wedding. She and her husband attended my son Neel's wedding. We meet each other occasionally.

She considers me as her elder brother and respects Manju and me accordingly. She talks to us about her family issues. We always care for each other's well-being.

J. Gilbert D. Castro

**Figure 9.19:
Gilbert Castro.**

Our friendship started in late 1970s. At that time, we both were working for the Xerox Corporation, where Gil (Gilbert) was a test engineer and I was a product assurance specialist. He was running operational tests of the Xerox computer printer system at remote locations to duplicate customers' office environments. When the system failed, Gil provided failure data to me. I would then analyze the data, determine the root cause, and calculate the system failure rate.

I used this test data to eliminate the root cause by working with design and manufacturing engineers. We had to work closely to achieve the product goals.

While working closely, we respected each other's specialties and started becoming friends, despite several differences. He was of Mexican descent. I was Indian. He was Catholic. I was Hindu. He lived in a farmhouse on a big piece of land, and he raised cows, horses, pigs, and chickens. I was living in a suburban house. He was good at working with his hands. I was good at financing, accounting, income taxes, bookkeeping, computers, and number crunching. However, we had a natural affinity for each other, and we became close friends for life.

As we started becoming close friends and trusting each other, he invited me to participate in his mini-warehouse project in Lewisville, Texas. (See chapter 8.3 for details.) I accepted his invitation and became his business partner, and we created the Gilval Partnership. He owned 75 percent, and I owned 25 percent of the partnership.

The mini-warehouse project was a successful real estate venture. It had excellent positive cash flow and big capital appreciation. The mini-warehouse project was a shining example of a business partnership based on friendship, trust, and mutual respect.

Gil and his wife, Charlotte, used the mini warehouses' cash flow to construct a big lakefront home in Little Elm, Texas. We also bought one hundred acres of adjoining land for investment purposes. Charlotte had a very high-level job in a bank with a good salary. Everything was cruising great. Suddenly, Charlotte lost her job. For Gil, the cash flow from the mini warehouses was not enough to make the mortgage payments on the big house and the land. He requested me, for my agreement, to sell the mini warehouses and let the land go back to the seller. He also sold the new house and moved to a smaller house. We made a good profit when we sold the mini warehouses. However, some of the capital gains got stuck in the seller-financed note.

I wished, at that time, that I'd had the capital to buy Gil's partnership and continue the mini warehouses and land ownership.

As soon as the seller-financed note got cashed out and we got our profit from the mini warehouses, Gil decided to build the big house of his dreams, on a big piece of land in Taylor, Texas. His house had a very impressive setting. He had a driveway that was more than a quarter-mile long, and a big water fountain in front of the house, with a circular driveway in front of the house's entrance. It was decorated with a Western theme. Behind the house, a quarter-mile away, he built a barn for horses, a garage for two horse-driven stagecoaches, storage, and a work area. Gil and Charlotte were enjoying their retirement in a luxurious dream home until a tragedy struck. Gil was diagnosed with pancreatic cancer. So sad! He was heartbroken, and so was I. Why should such punishment befall a nice, healthy, hardworking gentleman?

The cancer treatment required frequent trips to Dallas hospitals. Once he found out that the chances were low for his recovery, he decided to sell his dream home and moved to Murphy, Texas, an easy commuting distance to the Dallas hospitals.

Despite his physical condition, he and Charlotte attended my son Neel's wedding. I recognized their presence at the wedding.

Once he became bedridden, I visited him several times. I could not imagine him bedridden. I always saw him as being full of energy and doing things. That was a sharp turn in his life. The worse thing was that there was no cure for his cancer, and nobody could help him. The day before his death, his son called me and asked me to come and say goodbye to my close friend. For me, this was the most painful visit. When we used to meet, we would always kid and tease each other and laugh. I thanked him for the wonderful memories of our friendship. He murmured something. I felt that I was losing my brother.

His son requested me to give a eulogy at his funeral, which I did. My eulogy highlighted that our relationship was unique. It showed how two coworkers, who had never met each other before, became close friends, developed mutual respect and trust, became business partners, and remained friends for life.

Gil's departure created a big void in my life. Every time I must do something complicated with my hands, I remember him. I say to myself, *If Gil was alive, he would help me.*

K. Drs. Sitha and Krishna Babu

The Babus are our "made in America" friends. I met them when I was elected as first VP of the DFW Hindu Temple Society and Sithaji was elected as second VP. We worked together for the growth of the DFW Hindu Temple Society and to build a Hindu temple in the Dallas-Fort Worth metroplex area.

When I was president of the DFW Hindu Temple Society, Sithaji was the first VP of the society.

Figure 9.20: Drs. Sitha and Krishna Babu.

At that time, my temporary work assignment was in Austin, Texas. I was in Austin Monday through Friday. Sithaji, as the VP of the DFW Hindu Temple Society, took care of day-to-day operational issues of the temple that required the president's presence.

We had similar opinions on Hindu religious, social, and political issues. Not only that, but we also had one more common trait: we all three were highly educated with PhD degrees. These factors helped us to become close friends.

We participated together in the DFW Hindu Temple Society activities. We helped each other during important events of our lives such as birthday parties, graduation parties, and weddings. We took several cruises and land tours together.

Our relationship is more than just a close friendship. Sithaji became like a sister to me. She adopted me as a *rakhi* brother. We celebrated every Raksha Bandhan elaborately while they were living in the Dallas-Fort Worth area. After they moved to Houston, Texas (near their son), we continued to keep close contact and meeting each other.

Our friendship was unique and natural. I did not know them earlier. The DFW Hindu Temple Society brought us together. Mutual respect, honesty, and not expecting anything were key to our lifelong friendship.

L. Gita Forum Founding Families

We did not know any one of them, except Mathur Mori, before we moved to the Dallas area. We were fortunate to be a part of the Gita Forum's (see Chapter 12.1) founding families. It was created to cater to our religious needs and our desire to pass Hinduism to our kids. Since it was based on the common interests of families with similar backgrounds, it created a unique binding force. As a result, the Gita Forum became a well-recognized, close-knit organization in the Dallas metropolitan area.

Manju and I are thankful to the following Gita Forum founding families for enriching our lives and giving us pride and joy in living in the Dallas-Fort Worth area:

- Dr. Hasmukh and Dr. Indiraben Shah
- Ramanbhai and Shardaben Patel
- Rashmibhai and Smrutiben Shah
- Mathur and Vijuben Mori
- Bhoginbhai and Taruben Modi

9.6 INSPIRING TEACHERS AND PROFESSORS

Other people who enriched and shaped my life were my teachers and professors, starting from elementary school and through middle school, high school, junior college, engineering college, and my postgraduate education. They were there to instill knowledge in me and at the same time reform my outlook, character, and personality to fit the cultured and modern society, to get an education, and eventually, to get transplanted in America.

Since I was a smart student, got excellent grades, was always top of the class, was well-behaved, and respected authority, most of the teachers and professors liked my attitude, behavior, and good grades. I was one of their favorite students. Some of them took the extra step to help me with my personal situations. The following section contains a few examples of such help.

A. Strict First-Grade Teacher

My first-grade teacher was extremely strict, and he believed in disciplining the students by beating and other physical punishments. At that time, I didn't appreciate it, but now I think my being obedient and respecting authority during the rest of the school years must have come from my strict first-grade teacher.

B. Timekeeper Teacher

My middle-school teacher knew that I must leave my last class ten minutes before the end of the school day to catch the return train to my hometown.

He knew that I did not have a watch, so he would come to me and tell me that it was time to leave. What an unforgettable kindness!

C. Professors Helping with Transplantation

When I started applying for admission to American universities, I didn't understand all the terminology of the applications. My American-educated engineering college professors helped me to understand and fill out the applications, got them typed by their secretaries, wrote strong recommendation letters, and helped me to select the university to go to.

10

NURTURING NEXT GENERATIONS

10.1 PRIDE OF PARENTING NEHA AND NEEL

Parenting Neha and Neel was a unique experience full of joy, self-satisfaction, and challenges. Since Manju and I both were raised in India, we did not know about raising children in America. Neither our parents nor any relatives were in America to guide us at that time. We had a few friends with small children, so we learned a little bit from them and the rest from trial and error. Our home atmosphere was a mixed bag of Indian and American cultures. We developed a new Americanized Indian culture. For young children, it was tough to grow up in a dual culture. However, we tried our best to give them the best of both cultures. We instilled a good value system in their characters: to be honest, not to take undue advantage of others, to be hardworking, aim high, get a good education, and not spend beyond one's means. Besides these values, we provided them with a loving, caring, inspiring, and stable family environment.

Neha and Neel both knew my family roots and what it took to raise my living standard from an ordinary farming family in India to the level of an upper-middle-class American family. They knew that one of the key elements for my success in

Figure 10.1: Neha and Neel, 1975.

America was education. Therefore, both always focused on education. As a result, both achieved their career goals of becoming doctors.

I was busy advancing in my technical career when they were young. Manju decided to be a full-time mother to take care of them. When they were young, I was paying back my loans in India and providing money for improving the living standards of my family in India. This did not leave huge resources for Neha and Neel during their childhood. However, we provided all the necessities an upper-middle-class family could provide. Both were exceptionally good kids. They never demanded anything beyond our means.

Neha was born on October 27, 1966, when we were living in the Ivy Hill Apartments in Newark, New Jersey. Since she was our first child, everything she did was exciting and new to us. We started enjoying a new phase of our life together.

Neha was smart in school, and she was a loving and careful girl. She made many friends while she was in school and college.

Neel was born on November 22, 1968, when we were living in Parsippany, New Jersey. Since Neel was our second child, we knew some basics of raising a child.

Neel was a curious, adventurous, and daring boy. He made friends easily. He loved outside activities, such as riding his tricycle, sledding in the snow, going down the hill on a toy scooter, etc. When he was two years old, he wanted to be either a garbage man or a fireman. When he was in third grade, he wanted to be a surgeon.

When Neha and Neel were toddlers, we used to live in a garden apartment. Both shared a bedroom. They were very good-mannered kids and never had any fights, arguments, or sibling rivalries. When we moved to Plano, Texas, in a house, they each got their own bedroom.

As Neha and Neel moved from elementary school to middle and high school, their involvement in school and extracurricular activities kept changing. Neha participated in Girl Scouts, girls' soccer, ballet, viola classes, etc. Neel participated in Indian Guides (Adventure Guides), boys' soccer, Boy Scouts, and viola classes. I tried to take an active part in their extracurricular activities. I attended most of their soccer games, Indian Guide camps, recitals, soapbox car derbies, etc. I also played tennis with them for a brief period.

Since we were in the first wave of Indian immigrants (1960s), there were not that many Indian functions and cultural events to expose them to Indian culture at an early age. Many Indian immigrants came in the 1980s and 1990s, which brought many Indian culture-related activities and facilities. Many Indian families chose to raise their children in the Indian culture. We never forced Indian culture and Hindu religion on their personalities.

We visited India several times when they were growing up. We wanted them to bond with their grandparents and other relatives on both sides. They both enjoyed the visits, met relatives, explored India and Indian culture, and tried hands-on farming. They saw the place where I was born and raised. They understood where I was as a child and what it took to be in America.

When Neha was a teenager, she did not follow American culture and did not get involved with boys. We were happy and proud of her behavior at that time. However, we think it was our mistake not to encourage her to date and explore boys. When we realized our mistake, it was too late.

She was a sweet, smart, and satisfied girl. She never demanded anything too much. We gave her our old Dodge Dart when she was in high school. She never complained about it. However, when she graduated from the University of Texas at Austin, we gave her a new Nissan Maxima as a graduation gift and for going to medical school.

It was a different story with Neel. He was a very sociable person with many friends and girlfriends in high school and college. We gave him the freedom to do whatever he liked, as long as he kept good grades.

Neel loved cars. We gave him our old Dodge Dart when he started driving. He installed a high-power stereo system. He did not want his friends to see him driving an old clunker, so he used to park away from the high school. When the car got towed away for illegal parking, we felt bad and bought him a sporty-looking Chevrolet Monte Carlo.

Neel was a very bright student and a people person. When he was in his senior year of high school, he loved to go out with his friends and did not return past midnight. I used to worry a lot and waited for him in the game room. I could not sleep until he returned.

Once he went to college, we had no control over his social life and stopped worrying about him. We told him to do whatever he liked if he maintained good grades. He maintained excellent grades and secured admission to medical school. We were proud of his achievements.

Figure 10.2: Neha and Neel, 1992.

Having both kids in medical school was the proudest moment of our lives. All the friends, relatives, and coworkers used to ask us, "How did you do it?" We had no definite answer. We never pushed them to go to medical school. They were very smart and motivated kids. They knew the value of education in being successful early in life. We actively participated in their education and provided a stable, loving family environment, encouragement, and needed financial support. Like any other parents, we wanted them to be successful and happy in their chosen professions.

Seeing both the kids successfully settle down in their chosen professions is the most gratifying mission of our lives. Only a few lucky parents have such a fortune.

10.2 WELCOMING CHARLOTTE COOPER INTO THE DHUDSHIA FAMILY

When Neel finished medical school and started his residency, Manju and I tried to find a suitable match for him from our circle of family and friends. We passed on a few girls' biodata to Neel. But it did not produce any desirable results. We left Neel to find a suitable life partner.

After Neel finished his residency, he found Charlotte while he was doing his fellowship in Memphis, Tennessee, and she was a nurse. We were excited and thrilled that Neel had found someone he liked. We met her for the first time in Memphis, and we were impressed by her very courteous manner, education, smartness, cultured family background, and love for Neel. Our attitude was that whomever Neel liked, we would like. We met her again in Memphis and Plano. Her continued cheerful outlook about becoming a member of the Dhudshia family made us very comfortable.

Once Neel and Charlotte got engaged and moved to Las Vegas, I had several occasions to meet her there. I always wondered what was going through her mind as she was about to marry an Indian man. She had the courage and guts to come out of her comfort zone and take a chance.

We formally welcomed her into the Dhudshia family at their wedding in Las Vegas on May 27, 2006.

Figure 10.3: Charlotte and Neel, August 2006.

Since we had a large circle of family and friends in the Dallas area, we also wanted to have a Hindu wedding ceremony and reception there. Neel and Charlotte welcomed the idea and cooperated at every step. Manju and I planned and executed the event with some help from family and friends. Charlotte's family participated in the Hindu rituals, ceremonies, and customs wholeheartedly. Most of the ladies on the bride's side wore Indian saris. They all energetically participated in *ras* and garba (Indian folk dancing) until midnight.

At this wedding, we observed a blending of two cultures.

Once Charlotte and Neel settled down in life, we appreciated her love and respect. They are managing their affairs and raising their family. We assured Charlotte that we would be there wherever and for whatever help she may need.

To Manju and me, Charlotte is our second daughter. We care for her as much as we do for Neha.

10.3 BECOMING A GRANDPARENT

Becoming grandparents was another gratifying moment in our lives. We assume everybody loves to have grandchildren while they are in good health and can play with them. We are no different. We were patiently waiting for a long time to enter a new phase of our lives: becoming grandparents.

We love being grandparents and enjoying children without any responsibility. Once we became grandparents, our attitudes toward children changed drastically. Their shouting, crying, running around, and making a mess do not bother us anymore. On the contrary, they give us delightful feelings.

It is unfortunate that, because of distance and our active life in Dallas, we cannot be with them for a longer time to help them to grow and participate in their growing activities.

Our travels to Las Vegas have become more frequent. We made sure that we celebrate Christmas with them every year after the first grandchild. We visit at least one more time during the year. They also visit us in Plano at least once a year. These occasions help us bond with them.

A. First Grandchild: Austin

Figure 10.4: Austin Grace Dhudshia.

When Neel and Charlotte announced that they were expecting their first baby, Manju and I both were thrilled.

After Austin was born, we flew to Las Vegas as soon as she came home.

Since Austin was my first grandchild, her birth was a special event in my life. Seeing Austin for the first time and holding her in my hands was a thrilling experience. It felt like a jolt of electricity went through my body. I was trembling. What a wonderful experience to hold my first grandchild in hands for the first time! I instantly bonded with her. She created a special place in my heart forever.

Austin's birth brought back all the memories of our first child.

B. Second Grandchild: Abigail

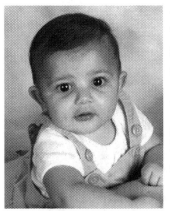

After Austin's birth, we were ready to welcome a second grandchild. Abigail's birth gave us one more star in our grandparents crowns.

What a wonderful experience to hold a grandchild in your hands for the first time! I instantly bonded with her. She also created a special place in my heart forever.

Figure 10.5: Abigail Dhudshia.

C. Third Grandchild: Cooper

We did not expect Charlotte and Neel would try for a third child. They surprised us with the news that they were expecting a boy, a third child. Having a boy in the family completed the family structure. We were overjoyed.

Figure 10.6: Cooper Dhudshia.

11

PAYING BACK

11.1 To Adopted Motherland

A. Monetary Help

While establishing roots in the adopted motherland, I became aware of my obligations to her through my employers' participation in the United Way programs. I became a regular donor to United Way through a direct donation deduction from my paycheck. Manju also started contributing through her employer. Once we got more familiar with the adopted motherland, we started donating money once a year to the following charitable organizations that we liked:

- St. Jude's Children's Research Hospital, Memphis, Tennessee: Finds cures for children with cancer and other catastrophic diseases through research and treatment.
- Meals on Wheels, McKinney, Texas: Provides warm and healthy meals to lonely homebound seniors.
- American Red Cross: Brings shelter, food, and comfort to those affected by disasters.
- ASME Foundation, New York, New York: Funds and develops programs that support, create, and advance the field of engineering.
- UNICEF, New York, New York: Delivers the essentials that give every child an equitable chance in life for health care and

immunizations, safe water and sanitation, nutrition, education, emergency relief, and more.

When we had to take minimum required distributions from our IRAs and our income rose to a comfortable level, we started donating sizable amounts directly from our IRAs to the following local organizations that were helping the local community's needs:

- Genesis Women's Shelter and Support, Dallas, Texas: Family violence shelter and services.
- Girls Inc. of Metropolitan Dallas, Texas: Inspires all girls to be strong, smart, and bold.
- North Texas Food Bank, Plano, Texas: Provides access to daily meals for hungry children, seniors, and families.

B. AARP Foundation Tax-Aide Volunteering

I became a member of the American Association of Retired Persons (AARP) when I turned sixty. I've always had an affinity for preparing income taxes by myself. Initially, I used to do the income tax returns manually. Later, I started using TurboTax software. At this point, I helped other family members to prepare their income taxes. When I retired from Texas Instruments Inc. on April 25, 2001, I wanted to use my knowledge for the local community's good. The AARP Foundation's Volunteer Income Tax Assistance (VITA) program came to my attention in June 2002, and I signed up to be a volunteer for the next tax season. This program is a cooperative effort of three participating organizations: (i) IRS, which provides computers, software, training, certification, internet, and printing hardware; (ii) AARP, which provides manpower made of retirees like me; and (iii) the City of Plano, which provides room at a local library. This volunteer work turned out to be important to keep my brain active and sharp. It gave me some structured activity in the local senior community. Every year, I go through training for tax law changes, new software usage, and the certification process. The training starts in January, and the tax filing season starts on February 1 and runs through April 15 of the tax year. This way, my first quarter of the calendar year is busy with tax volunteering. I get self-satisfaction for helping all sorts of people, mostly retired elderly people. Their heartfelt thanks have kept me going to help them year after year since 2002.

11.2 FOR IMPROVING FAMILY ECONOMIC CONDITION

A. Economic Conditions before I Came to America

Looking at my current family condition in America, no one can guess that I was a son of an ordinary farmer in India who owned less than twelve acres of land and a one-room house in a small village, without running water and electricity. My parents lived a basic and simple life: plain and cheap food and clothes, and a crowded house without any furniture or luxury items. They used to get up at 4:00 a.m. to milk buffaloes, clean barns, and cook and feed family members. After finishing the morning chores, my mother worked on farms all day. At night, she took care of the family dinner and the kids. Their workday used to end at 10:00 p.m. With hard work, they did succeed a bit. However, raising seven children drained all the resources they created. My parents had no sure way to uplift the living standard. My parents encouraged my eldest brother, Vithal, to go to Africa. He did not take the opportunity. My parents bought a partnership in a business with their life's savings. The other partner cheated, and my parents were forced to pull out with a big loss. My brother Devraj tried his luck and went to Kolhapur to get into some business there. He could not take the separation from his family, and he came back. All my parents' efforts to elevate our family's living standards did not bring any significant improvement.

B. After I Came to America

My becoming an engineer and coming to America drastically changed the living standard of my family in India. During the first ten years of my living in America, I sent most of my savings to my parents, my brother Devraj, and my sisters. We lived in America tightfisted and saved money for uplifting the living standard of my family in India. One of my goals in coming to America was to uplift my family's living standard in India. With my monetary support and my parents' and brother Devraj's hard work, they bought more farmland, raised a mango orchard, bought a partnership in a raw sugar factory, renovated the old house into a seven-room residence, educated kids, bought luxury items, and started enjoying very comfortable upper-middle-class life in India with electricity, TV, telephone, good food, clothing, medical care, a motorcycle, a car, servants, and a high status in the society.

After I became an American citizen, I applied for and got approval for immigration visas (green cards) for all my siblings. Only my brother Devraj and sister Anjani took advantage of immigrating to America. When my brother Devraj came to America and received a green card, I applied for an immigration visa for both of his sons, Raju and Anil. After their applications got approved, my brother decided to send only one son, Anil, to America. Anjani, her husband, Chimanlal, and her sons, Amul and Digant, came to America together. At that time, Neha and Neel were in high school. We were not used to having nine people in one house. However, we all sacrificed many personal things to help them settle in America, and we put them on a path to independent living. We kept Amul and Digant with us for six more months to teach them the American language and manners. We also kept Anil living with us for a while. Before he got comfortable with the odd job and free living, I encouraged him to join the University of Texas at Arlington (UTA) for further education. At that time, I was a part-time adjunct professor at UTA. I am glad he joined UTA and graduated with a computer science degree.

To elevate the living standard of my family in India to the upper-middle-class level and settle all my relatives who had immigrated to America required lots of understanding, support, sacrifices, and cooperation from my life partner, Manju, and my kids Neha and Neel. Without their support, I could not have done whatever I did for my family in India and my relatives in America. There was neither social nor religious pressure to do anything for them. But I had a moral obligation to do whatever was required to improve their economic conditions. Manju and I did it, to the best of our ability, at our own will, and for our own personal satisfaction.

We are happy that we were capable and willing to do our best to uplift the economic condition of my family in India and whoever immigrated to America. This was my father's dream: to get out of laborious farming and poverty.

11.3 TO BIRTH MOTHERLAND: INDIA

When I reflect and think about my growing up in India, I feel that I got lots of help from Mother India. I received a free primary, middle school, and high school education. The Government of India subsidized my junior college and engineering college. Their tuition fees were minimal, and on top of that, the Indian government gave me scholarships at both colleges.

While growing up, health care was free.

I also got financial help from the following regional Kadwa Patidar community during my college study in India:

- Amrutbai Scholarship for junior college
- Patel Mohanlal Gokaldas Scholarship for engineering college

When I sum it up, I feel that I owe a lot to Mother India and the Kadwa Patidar community.

It is always in my mind how to pay them back. I started contributing to every opportunity I could get to help Indian citizens during natural disasters and health issues. To mention a few:

- When the flood destroyed Javahar Vinay Mandir High School, in my hometown of Shapur, during the monsoon on June 22, 1983, I organized a fundraising event in the Dallas area, with the help of Gita Forum members, and raised funds for rebuilding four classrooms of the high school.
- My brother Devraj and I bought a small piece of land right across from the railway station for future commercial use. Once I decided not to live in India, we sold the land and donated the proceeds to

Javahar Vinay Mandir High School, in memory of my father, to build a wing that houses science labs. This donation honors my father's vision to escape from poverty through education.

- While helping my family in India, I paid back Kadwa Patidar scholarship providers.

- Once my family obligations slowed down and I was ready to pay back my scholarship from the Government of India, I could not because the department was closed and there was not any department that was equivalent to it. Instead, I took indirect ways to pay back.

- When we had to take the minimum required distribution from our IRAs and our income rose to a comfortable level, we also started donating sizable amounts to the Kadwa Patel Samaj of North America (KPSNA).

11.4 TO HINDUISM

I am a Hindu but I am not an old-fashioned religious person. I do not place blind faith in some of the Hindu religious rituals. However, I admire many teachings of Hinduism. I did whatever was needed to: (i) preserve the Hindu religious culture; (ii) help Hindus in the Dallas-Fort Worth area to unite; and (iii) build awareness of the greatness of the Hindu religion among non-Hindu communities.

Once my family got stable after our move to the Dallas area, we started paying attention to our need to get connected with our religion of Hinduism. That led us to form the Gita Forum (see chapter 12.1). When the Gita Forum became a mature organization, all the members saw a need to expand and get connected to a larger Hindu community residing in the Dallas area. This led to the formation of the DFW Hindu Temple Society (see chapter 12.2).

To establish and run the DFW Hindu Temple Society, I volunteered lots of time and donated a sizable amount of funds. Once the temple got off the ground, I continued participating in the executive committee and became president and a member of the board of trustees. I also continued donating money to the temple as needed.

As a result of dedicated volunteer services and generous donations of many Hindu devotees, the temple became a well-established Hindu religious center in the Dallas-Fort Worth area. I continued volunteering my time and donating, as detailed in chapter 12.2.

12

COMMUNITY AND PROFESSIONAL LINKAGES

12.1 GITA FORUM

In 1977, ten Gujarati families living in Dallas, Texas, areas decided to do something for their children to make them aware of Hindu culture and religion. We started reading the Gita (the most sacred book of the Hindu religion) every month at one of our homes. Slowly, we increased our activities to include the celebration of Janmashtami (Lord Krishna's birthday), Navratri ras/garba (folk dance), Diwali (the Hindu New Year), and family outings at Texas state parks, mostly Tyler State Park in Tyler, Texas. At the same time, our circle increased to more than twenty families. At that point, we started using the recreation center in Richardson, Texas, for our monthly meetings. The Gita Forum received recognition as a well-organized association of highly qualified and dedicated professionals. We helped anyone in social need (such as at times of death, weddings, birthdays, graduations, etc.) in the Dallas area. We generated funds by selling Coke and hotdogs at Cotton Bowl Stadium. In 1979, we tried to buy an old church in Farmers Branch but could not, due to a lack of required capital. We decided to enlarge our circle and invited other people to join the group. Dallas Hindu community leaders met at Raman Patel's home to unite and buy the church. By the time we united, the church had been sold. Out of these enlargement efforts, the DFW Hindu Temple Society was born. We continued to operate as the Gita Forum and provided leadership to the bigger organization, the DFW Hindu Temple Society.

As soon as the DFW Hindu temple was built in Irving, Texas, Gita Forum members started having differences of opinion to move the monthly meetings to the Hindu temple. It got split: half of them decided to move to the Hindu temple and the other half decided to continue as before, outside the temple. We went with the group that went to the Hindu temple. Later, it was renamed Gita Sanskar. They continued reading Gita at the Hindu temple on the third Saturday of every month.

Association with the Gita Forum gave us pride and joy while living in the Dallas-Fort Worth area. We learned a lot about Gita and the Hindu religion. Not only that, but it also gave us many learning opportunities for social and leadership skills through organizing and executing community and social events. Being a homogenous and cohesive group, social bonding among members and their kids was easy. The Gita Forum provided leadership and grassroots support to establish, manage, and grow the DFW Hindu Temple Society.

Another noticeable long-term benefit of the Gita Forum, to the Gita Forum members' kids, is that most of them are successful professionals in their chosen fields.

12.2 DFW HINDU TEMPLE SOCIETY

My association with the DFW Hindu Temple Society (HTS) started before it was formed. I'd found an old church for sale in Farmers Branch that the Gita Forum wanted to buy. However, the Gita Forum could not raise enough funds for the purchase. Some of the Gita Forum members decided to enlarge the Gita Forum and go outside the group to solicit funds. That led to the formation of the DFW HTS. By the time the DFW HTS was loosely organized, the property had been sold. In 1983, the DFW HTS was formally organized, and I became a founding member of the society.

I was elected (selected) for the DFW HTS executive committee in 1988. The DFW HTS elected me as the treasurer of the society in 1989 and 1990. In 1991, I entered the chain of presidential candidates, starting as a second vice president, then as first vice president in 1992, and president in

1993. After a two-year break, I served on the DFW HTS board of trustees, as a trustee of the society, for six years (two three-year terms), two of which I served as the secretary of the board.

As mentioned in the previous section, I am a Hindu, but I am not an old-fashioned religious person who places blind faith in some of the Hindu religious rituals. My main goals to associate with the DFW HTS were: (i) to preserve the Hindu religious culture for my future generations, (ii) to help Hindus in the Dallas-Fort Worth area to unite, (iii) to build awareness of the greatness of the Hindu religion among non-Hindu communities, (iv) to make good use of my spare time for the Hindu community, and (v) to have a place for worship and get-togethers. While I was active in temple management, I was invited to speak about the Hindu religion at several local community colleges, churches, and other civic organizations. I prepared a PowerPoint presentation about the basics of the Hindu religion (Hinduism 101) and used it for my talks.

The DFW HTS gave me opportunities to help Hinduism. Not only that, but my association with the DFW HTS also broadened my horizon a lot. I learned a lot about dealing with and working with all kinds of people, Hindus, and non-Hindus. I met many good people and made many good, lifetime friends. I modernized the temple management operations using modern business techniques. I introduced the use of computers for maintaining the financial accounts books. I changed the way the temple management was conducting the executive committee, board of trustees, and general body meetings by using visual aids, following structured agendas, and creating a disciplined meeting environment.

12.3 DALLAS INDIAN LIONS CLUB

In the early 1990s, a few well-to-do Indian professionals living in the Dallas-Fort Worth metroplex area wanted to do something for the non-Indian community. Ideas to form the Dallas Indian Lions Club came from this desire. A group of twenty-five professionals got together and approached the Lions Club International headquarters for a permit and help to open a local chapter in the Dallas-Fort Worth metroplex area.

The idea was welcomed, and the new Lions Club chapter, the Dallas Indian Lions Club, was established with a gala opening celebration on June 15, 1995. I was one of the twenty-five charter members. Manju and other members' wives performed Indian folk dances at the charter night celebration.

The club met once a month for dinner and has a gala fundraising dinner every year. The club did a lot of charity work and gave scholarships to high school graduates. I remained a regular member for four years, and when I moved away to the DFW Hindu Temple Society, I only participated in the yearly gala fundraising dinners.

12.4 INTEREST GROUPS

A. Investment Club

At one of the social gatherings of close friends living around Plano in 2009, discussions were on several odd topics, as usual. But on this day, Rashmibhai Shah came up with a suggestion to form an investment club. Some of us had been part of an investment club in the 1980s. Because a few members had moved out of the Dallas area, that club was dissolved. We thought it was a great idea. On that day, nine individuals committed to becoming members of the proposed investment club. I prepared the bylaws for the Gita Investment Club Partnership, got a tax ID, and registered the club with the State of Texas. I was selected by the club members to be the treasurer. I opened a broker account at Fidelity Investments and received initial invested checks from the partners. Initially, all partners contributed $25,000 each. We started the Gita Investment Club in June 2009.

Subsequently, the club added two more partners, and one dropped out. In the end, we had ten partners. Initially, the club started investing in individual stocks. Later, the investment mix was more ETFs.

In 2019, the club reached a major milestone of becoming a million-dollar club. Most of the time, the club performed better than the S&P 500 index.

The atmosphere of the club operations was friendly, cooperative, and accommodating. All the members had one goal in mind: to make a wise investment in the stocks and have fun while doing it. The club had the benefits of varied opinions, lots of research, discussions, and different ideas about where to invest. Most of the time, every member agreed to the decisions made for the investment. There was a lot of learning about selecting investment ideas which could be used for personal portfolios, too.

Association with the investment club had several other benefits, such as club-sponsored cruises and dinners with family.

B. Bridge Group

I was always attracted to playing bridge, a card game. Bridge requires lots of logic, memory, and planning strategy. I had read several instruction books and started playing with close friends in the 1970s. It did not work out. I gave up. However, after I retired, an opportunity came to be a member of a bridge group. I took the challenge, relearned the game, and started playing with the expert players, Rashmi Shah, Jyoti Bhatia, and Vijai Jain. They were kind to accommodate my skill level and teach me proper techniques. We four started the bridge group in early 2009. On the way, we lost Jyoti Bhatia due to poor health and added two members, Harshad Parikh and Bhupen Shah. We play bridge every Thursday, from noon to 4:00 p.m., religiously. We take turns for who will host the game. The best part of the game is the tea break. The host always prepares the best snacks, sweets, and tea. It also gives us the opportunity to catch up with the Indian community and American political news during the break.

All the members always look forward to Thursday bridge sessions. Bridge gives me lots of pleasure and stimulation, and it keeps my mind sharp.

C. First-Friday Pizza Group

At one of the social gatherings of close friends living around Plano in 2008, discussions were on several odd topics, as usual. One of the topics was about getting tired of having Indian food at every social gathering. Instead, the group came up with a suggestion to form an interest group of pizza fans. The response was overwhelming, and an interest group was formed. The group agreed to meet on the first Friday of every month and have simple operations: one family would host the pizza party and would provide salad, drinks, and dessert. The host would also order the pizza and handle the payment, and whoever was in attendance would pay five dollars per person. This simple model of the pizza party has worked out great. It has freed up a host of cooking responsibilities. No need to have any formal invitation; it requires a simple email notification, and whoever can come is welcome. The participants enjoy food, friends' company, interesting discussions, and fellowship.

It has been functioning greatly since its inception. It has become a model pizza group in the Dallas metropolitan area.

D. Senior Lunch Group

The number of highly educated and successful senior male Indians in their seventies and eighties was growing in the Dallas metropolitan area in the early 2010s. Most of them were well-settled and were either retired or semi-retired. Once they had left their regular employment, they felt a need for a business lunch, which they used to have while working full-time. One of our friends, Mr. Baldev Patel, came up with an idea to get together to have lunch at a local restaurant and talk about the current business environment, stock market, other investment ideas, health insurance, health issues, or whatever was of interest to the attendees. The interested seniors agreed to meet at noon on the second Tuesday of the month. Mr. Baldev Patel volunteered to organize the group, send email notifications, and make a reservation at the local restaurant with a meeting room facility. Whoever wanted to attend the lunch would notify the organizer and show up. Each person would pay for their own lunch. Very simple organization operations!

It has been functioning greatly since its inception. It has become a model first-Tuesday senior lunch group in the Dallas metropolitan area.

E. Carpenter Recreation Center Morning Walking Buddies

Manju and I joined the Carpenter Recreation Center right after it opened in early 1991. Ever since, we have been members of the recreation center (except for one year). When I was working for Texas Instruments, either I was going to its fitness center at lunchtime or to the Carpenter Recreation Center after work. Since we went to the recreation center irregularly and at different times, we didn't get to know anyone closely.

When I retired from Texas Instruments, I started going to the Carpenter Recreation Center in the morning. And when Manju retired from Target, we both started going to the recreation center regularly in the morning. Seeing a familiar face every day changed the social dynamic. It started with morning greetings to familiar faces. Then it went further as we introduced each other by name and talked a little more about who we are. Eventually, we found out that we had many things in common, such as interests in exercising in the morning, being retired high-level employees of the local big employers (like Texas Instruments, JCPenney, Exxon, IBM, Bank of America, etc.), having grandchildren, and living independently in the neighborhood.

This created a very cordial social environment that made the morning walks very interesting. We had common topics to talk about while walking, depending on the day and the person we were walking with. Topics included health issues, home maintenance, grandkids, vacation plans, the current political environment, beliefs, jobs we had worked on, personal hobbies, etc.

These morning walks brought us closer and created bonds with others. We started having breakfast, lunch, and dinner gatherings at the local restaurants, as well as Christmas and birthday celebrations, etc.

The Carpenter Recreation Center morning walking buddies brought lots of joy of exercising into our lives.

12.5 PROFESSIONAL SOCIETIES

A. American Society of Mechanical Engineers (ASME)

When I started my master's in mechanical engineering, my adviser, Professor Budenholzer, encouraged me to join the ASME as a student member. At that time, he was in the leadership role of the Pressure Vessel Division of ASME. Once I started working at Foster Wheeler, my membership was upgraded to regular membership. At that time, I was very active in ASME: writing and reviewing research papers and using and improving the design and manufacturing process standards of the pressure vessels.

When I changed my job and started working for Xerox Corporation, the end product of my interest changed from pressure vessels to electromechanical systems. My new job did not require the latest developments in the mechanical engineering field. I had to lessen my ties with the ASME.

I continued my membership in the ASME while working for the Xerox Corporation and Texas Instruments. When I retired, I became an honorary member of the society.

I benefited a lot from my membership in the ASME. The ASME Foundation is one of the major beneficiaries of my monetary donations. The focus of the foundation is to encourage high school students to choose careers in engineering.

B. American Society for Quality (ASQ)

After I joined the Xerox Corporation, my job focus changed to product reliability assurance. I looked for a professional society membership to enhance my knowledge about product reliability. At that time, there were none. However, the American Society for Quality had a division for reliability. So, I became a member of ASQ and joined its Reliability Division. Soon after that, I became an active member of the Reliability Division. As an active member, I attended all the annual reliability and maintainability symposiums and the annual quality congress.

When I joined Texas Instruments, my job focus remained on product reliability. Therefore, I continued my membership in the ASQ.

The Malcolm Baldridge National Quality Award, a joint recognition program of the ASQ and the US Department of Commerce, selected me, for two years, as an examiner for the award.

Since I was volunteering for ASQ activities and was actively engaged in the betterment of the product reliability technology, the ASQ bestowed upon me ASQ fellow recognition on November 19, 1998.

C. Semiconductor Equipment and Materials International (SEMI)

When I started working for Texas Instruments (TI), my job focus changed to the reliability and maintainability of semiconductor manufacturing equipment. Once I settled down in my new job, my supervisor gave me the responsibility to represent TI in the SEMI committee that was standardizing the semiconductor manufacturing equipment performance metrics. This responsibility became a stepping stone for me to be an active member of the committee. Since I had an extensive background in reliability and maintainability, I promptly became a prominent member of the committee. My ideas were widely used to prepare a SEMI specification, SEMI E-10, entitled *Guideline for Definition and Measurement of Equipment Reliability and Maintainability (RAM)*. Eventually, I was recognized as a SEMI E-10 expert in semiconductor manufacturing equipment manufacturers and users. Later, SEMI requested me to volunteer to conduct SEMI E-10 seminars at SEMICON West, SEMICON Japan, SEMICON Singapore, and SEMICON Europa.

My association with SEMI gave me an excellent opportunity to shine in the industry. I gained lots of practical knowledge in the reliability discipline, and that encouraged me to write my book, *Hi-Tech Equipment Reliability*.

The committee and the SEMI members recognized my contributions and bestowed me with several awards and the nickname of Mr. Reliability.

I continued active participation in the committee until 2021.

13

PIVOTAL POINTS THAT COULD HAVE CHANGED THE COURSE OF MY LIFE

13.1 PERSONAL CHOICES

A. Quitting School after Fourth Grade

When I completed the fourth grade, I did not go to school after the summer vacation. Instead, I started helping my uncle Bhovan on the farms, particularly watering the sugar cane farms. He liked my help, and I liked the freedom. I loved eating fresh farm produce like mangoes, sugar cane, cucumbers, mung beans, carrots, onions, etc. I could have been a fourth grade-educated farmer for the rest of my life, if the following incident had not happened.

Right after summer vacation, my fourth-grade teacher (who was then a fifth-grade teacher) met my father in the Shapur market area and asked my father about my not continuing school. He told my father, "Vallabh was a very bright student (first in the fourth grade), and why is he not continuing his education?" My father did not know anything about my not continuing my education. Since I was a member of a large, joint family, he never noticed my not going to school.

But that evening, when I returned from the farms on the bullock cart with my uncle, my father caught me by my ear and shook me, and he asked me, "Why are you not going to school?"

I told him, "I like farming with my uncle and do not want to go to school."

Soon after that, he became calm and started reasoning with me. He took me aside and said, "Son, you cannot prosper in this world without education. You must have a good education to succeed in this world. Look at your uncle Jasmat. How much did he prosper with education? Your two elder brothers have already quit school and are now helping me on the farms. We do not need any extra help on the farms."

He insisted that I should go to school the next day. Since I did not have any clothes for school, he bought cloth material that evening, took it to our family tailor, and got one school dress stitched by the next day morning. He took me to school and reenrolled me in the fifth grade. My education restarted from that day onward without any stoppage, until I got my PhD.

At that time, I did not fully understand my father's insistence on education and the immense power of education. As I progressed through high school and college, I started understanding and appreciating it. Without my father's insistence, support, and vision, I would not have continued my education. I could have been an elementary school-educated poor farmer.

B. Going to Buniyadi-Style Schooling

When I completed sixth grade, I had to select a schooling style: (i) Stay with the Buniyadi-style schooling. This schooling style was based on Gandhi's nationalistic philosophy: no English language in the curriculum, treat everyone equally and with respect, serve the community, wear hand-spun fabric cloth only, reject foreign-made merchandise, etc., or (ii) Go to a bigger city and start a regular middle school with English in the curriculum.

I almost went to Buniyadi-style schooling. My father did not like that style. He encouraged me and helped me to join a regular middle school in the nearby big city. If I had not gone to a regular middle school, I would not have become an engineer. I could have been an activist for social equality.

C. Selecting Medical Profession

When I finished my first year of junior college, I had to select one of the two choices for the second-year curriculum. One choice included mathematics and physics courses that were required for admission into an engineering college. The other choice included biology and organic chemistry courses that were required for admission into a medical college. I could have selected either choice. I was good in either curriculum. There were no career advisers on campus. My parents did not have any preference. Since I loved mathematics and physics more than organic chemistry, I chose to take courses for admission to an engineering college. If I had taken another choice, I could have been a successful physician.

13.2 FAMILY SITUATIONS

A. Bother Vithal Sticking to Grocery Store Business

My father always looked for an opportunity to get out of farming. When I was in the fifth grade, our family bought a partnership interest in a small grocery store in Dhoraji, a good-size city twenty miles from my hometown. My eldest brother represented our business interest and worked there as a working partner. The business was going great. I spent one summer vacation there with my brother and helped him around the store and tending to its customers. I enjoyed the store's operations. I thought our family would be absorbed in it and would have an opportunity to get out of farming. But the circumstances changed. Another partner cheated us. He siphoned off cash and cooked the account books, and as a result, the store lost money. During an audit, my uncle found out that another partner was cheating. He conceded the cheating, offered to give up his partnership interest, and walked away. My brother did not have the guts to take full ownership and responsibility to operate the thriving grocery store. Instead, he walked away with little money in his hand. My family lost a big chunk of their savings. If my brother had taken full ownership and responsibility of the grocery store, I would have joined him after high school and would have become a grocery store owner/operator.

B. Brother Devraj Staying in Kolhapur and Getting into a Business

Since my eldest brother failed in the venture, my father wanted to give an opportunity to my elder brother Devraj to get out of farming. My uncle's acquaintance wanted to enlarge his business in Kohlapur, a big city almost one thousand miles from our hometown. My uncle recommended to my father to send my elder brother Devraj as an intern and then become a partner in their business. When I was in my first year of college, my elder brother went to Kohlapur. He became very proficient in business operations, learned the local language, and was ready to jump into the business. However, he could not take the family separation and the lonely lifestyle. He decided to come back and let the opportunity go. If he had stayed there, our family might have gone into business there and moved there.

14

TOP MEMORABLE EVENTS IN DETAIL

My life story is nothing but a sequence of numerous events. Some of them are memorable events that have stayed fresh in my memory. They have already been briefly covered earlier. However, they are detailed in the following sections.

14.1 ABUSING AND HUMILIATING ENCOUNTER

This encounter happened when I was around eight years old. My father and I were talking and walking on the main street of our town. At that time, our town was ruled by a Muslim king. The local Muslims were strict about respecting their mosque, which was located on the main street on which we were walking. Every man who walked in front of the mosque was required to take off his turban or cap, hold it in his hand, and pass the mosque in total silence. Since we were talking and walking, we did not realize that we were entering the mosque's silence zone. My father forgot to take off his turban, and I forgot to take off my cap. Soon after having gone about ten feet into the zone, a Muslim teenage boy noticed us, rushed to us, and stopped us. He shouted and told my father, "Hey, Patla [an insulting word for Patels], don't you know the rules in this zone?" He grabbed my father's turban and my cap, took them to the side, and peed on them. He brought them back and ordered us to wear them. Then he told us, " Next time you pass by this mosque, you will remember to take off your turban." I was horrified, and my father was shocked. An adult man had been insulted in front of his kid. How embarrassing! My father was so embarrassed, he did not speak a word to me for a long time. I could never forget this incident, even though the ruling Muslim king is gone, India became independent, and I do not live in that town. This incident gave me very long-lasting bad feelings about it.

14.2 TEMPORARY SHORT REFUGEE MIGRATION

When India became independent in 1947, two countries were created: India (with a Hindu majority) and Pakistan (with a Muslim majority). Many kings were given an opportunity to decide which country to align/ join with. Our Muslim king decided to join Pakistan, despite most of the population being Hindus. This was a very weird situation. A part of Pakistan was within India, like Dallas County became a part of Mexico. As soon as our kingdom became Pakistan, the cronies of the king started torturing the Hindu majority. They could take away from any Hindu family anything they liked, and they could order Hindus to do anything for them for free. This was like slavery. No one could say or do anything about it. If you complained, they would punish you and/or kill you. The worst thing they did was to take away beautiful young Hindu ladies and use them for their sexual pleasure. To escape from such torture, my family decided to send away all the young boys and girls to my eldest sister Shantaben's home in the town of Pipalia, in the neighboring Hindu kingdom, only twenty miles away.

At that time, I was in second grade. I did not comprehend the entire situation. My sister and her husband kept us with them. They had their own large family, and we were an added burden. I could never forget the kindness of my sister and her husband as they sheltered us in their home. I started second grade there in a very crowded and chaotic school. I did not learn much.

In 1948, a locally organized freedom fighter army, supported by the Indian Army, attacked the king, forced him to leave his kingdom, and freed the population to decide its own fate. Soon after the king left, the kingdom had a plebiscite about joining India. The population approved the alignment with India by a 95-percent favorable vote. As soon as our kingdom became part of India, all the Muslim terrorists and cronies left the kingdom, and we all came back to our homes. I restarted my second-grade education in my town.

14.3 PERSISTENT FATHER AND A LUCKY BREAK

As mentioned earlier in chapter 2.3, there was no middle school in Shapur. They had a seventh-grade class, but it did not have the English language in the curriculum. My father wanted me to go to a school where they had English in the curriculum. He then took me and my four classmates to Junagadh and tried to enroll us in City Middle School (Shree Narsinh Vidyamandir) near the railway station. We were denied admission because the Shapur school had a seventh grade.

My father didn't take the school principal's denial. He asked him, "Is there any way to circumvent the denial?"

The school principal told my father, "The only way to circumvent it is to make a special application to the school district's superintendent."

My father knew that the superintendent's office was about a mile away from the school. We didn't have much time, so we had to rush to the office.

We started a march (sort of) to the superintendent's office. It looked like a village man was leading a caravan of five teenage boys, laden with school bags, through the streets of the city of Junagadh. Everyone on our way was looking at us.

When we arrived at the superintendent's office, my father neither had any paper nor any pen to prepare the application. Luckily, there were paid street vendors who specialized in preparing the applications. He got the application prepared, paid one rupee to the vendor, and was ready to take it to the superintendent for his approval and signature. The doorman stopped us from going into the superintendent's office. He started arguing with my father about why he couldn't let us go inside the superintendent's office. (In reality, he wanted some money from my father.) While the argument was going on, the head clerk for the superintendent returned from lunch. Luckily, the head clerk happened to be our neighbor's son, who knew my father from his childhood. When he saw my father, he stopped and greeted him and asked what was going on. My father explained to him about the need for the school superintendent's approval and signature.

The clerk said, "Let me take care of it." He took the application from my father and told us to wait at the door.

Within ten minutes he came back with the school superintendent's approval stamp and signature. Then he told my father, "Whenever you need any help from this office, just ask for me." We all thanked him for his timely help and then thanked God for a lucky break. My father knew that such approval could take several days.

Once we got the approved application, we marched back to the middle school. While going back, we all were happy campers. When we arrived at the school, we were hungry and thirsty. My father bought half a dozen bananas from a street vendor in front of the school. We all had a banana for a late lunch.

After the short lunch break, my father took us to the school principal's office. He gave the approved application to the doorman and requested him to quickly take it to the principal.

Within a few minutes, the principal came out. He was surprised to see that the application had been approved in a very short time. The principal took us to his head clerk and asked him to enroll all of us boys in the seventh grade. The head clerk took our biodata and school-leaving certificates from the previous school and completed the official enrollment process.

Once the enrollment was completed, the head clerk took us to our assigned class. There were eight seventh-grade classes. I was assigned to class A. He took me to the class and told the teacher that I would be one of his students. The teacher welcomed me and introduced me to my classmates.

There were twenty boys in the class. They all were city boys. My outlook looked different from theirs. During the break between two periods, I thanked the classroom teacher and asked his permission to leave the class. My father was waiting outside. Once all five boys had returned from their classes, we went to the railway station and took the return train to my hometown.

When I reflect on this day, I see that it was one of the luckiest days of my life. What a lucky break we got! Normally, it could take several days to get the application approved by the school superintendent. With the lucky break, we got it approved within a few hours.

The more I think about it, the more I appreciate my father's persistence in providing me with an education.

14.4 GUTSY DECISION AND GODSENT HELP

When I was in eighth grade, we had only half-day school on Saturdays, from 8:00 a.m. to 11:00 a.m. To catch the 11:05 a.m. train to go back home, I had to leave my last class a little early and sprint to the railway station. On most Saturdays, I caught the train. But on one Saturday, I missed it by a few feet. I had been a little late. When I entered the train station, the train started moving. I ran as fast as I could, but the train picked up speed and I could not get on it. I ran all the way to the end of the platform and saw the train pulling out of the station. I stopped there and thought about what to do. I could wait for six hours for the next train, which was scheduled at 5:00 p.m., or I could walk seven miles to my home. If I started walking, I would reach my home in two hours. I made a gutsy decision to walk home. I told myself, *If there is a will, there is a way, and God will help me to finish my gutsy move.* Since I did not expect any train to come by until 5:00 p.m., I started walking on the railroad tracks. I was hungry and thirsty, but it did not matter. I must have walked about a mile from the station when I heard some mechanical noise. I noticed an open motorized carriage was coming from behind. I stepped away from the track and continued walking on the side strip. It was a railroad track inspector with his staff on board, and they were inspecting the tracks. I let them pass me. Once they passed me, a schoolboy walking with a school bag, they stopped, and the inspector asked me to come to him.

He asked me, "Where are you going?"

I told him, "I missed the train, and I am walking to my hometown, the next station."

He told me to get on his carriage and sit next to him on the front bench. The carriage had two other assistants on board who were inspecting the railway tracks.

Once the carriage started moving, the inspector asked me, "Are you hungry?"

I said, "Yes, a little bit."

So he gave me some snacks from his lunch box. Then he gave me some water to drink. After that, he asked me about my school, and he explained to me what he was inspecting. We talked about several other things before we reached my hometown's railway station. When they stopped at the station, I thanked them and got off the carriage. I was so happy to have reached my hometown station in a short time.

I started thinking about what had happened. Who had sent a kind and warmhearted railroad track inspector who gave me a ride on his carriage? That confirmed my belief that if you have guts, God will send help.

When I reached home, my mother was eagerly waiting and worrying for me. It had been about an hour since the train that I was supposed to be on had come by. My mother had expected me to be home a long time ago. At that time, there was not any way to communicate with my mother about missing the train. She was happy to see me back from school. She hugged me and thanked God that I had reached home safely. Then I told her what had happened. She also believed that God must have had something to do with sending the kind and warmhearted railroad track inspector to give me a ride.

14.5 First Thanksgiving in America

I did not know of any American holidays, including Thanksgiving, before I came to America. After I came to America and settled down in my studies, I started participating in the International Student Organization's activities on the IIT campus. With cooperation from the Chicago Foreign Student Association and local families in Danville, Illinois, they arranged a four-day Thanksgiving trip for foreign students at the IIT campus. I signed up for the fully paid trip. All the participants took a train from Chicago to Danville. This was my first experience riding on the American railways. When we arrived at the station in Danville, a large crowd of host families welcomed us and matched us to our assigned families. My host family was Dr. Robert Elghammer and Mrs. Doris Elghammer. They had three sons, a daughter, and a cat. They lived in a nice, big home with all the modern amenities. This was the first opportunity for me to see how a typical well-to-do American family lived in a suburb.

All the Elghammer family members welcomed me as a special guest into their family. They were eager to know about me and to tell me how they lived. The boys showed me their rooms with all their toys and sports paraphernalia. The girl showed me her room decorated as a princess's room. Everything I saw was new to me. Later, the little girl asked me where my feathers were (in reference to American Indians). I did not understand the question. Her mother clarified that I was an Indian from India and not an American Indian. At that time, I did not know anything about the American Indians. Mrs. Elghammer knew that I was a vegetarian, so she prepared all the meals accordingly. The first dinner with the family members was a special welcoming dinner. The variety of vegetarian dishes, prayer, formality, and discipline were very impressive. This dinner brought back my memories of family dinners in India.

After dinner, we talked quite a bit about India. Everybody was curious to know about India, and I was curious to know about the way American families lived.

On Thanksgiving Day, after breakfast, all the family members and I drove to Mrs. Elghammer's parents' home, about an hour away. They lived in a big farmhouse on a five hundred-acre farm. The house was surrounded by farms. However, it had all the amenities of a modern home in a big city. I met her parents, her brother and his wife, and her sister and her husband. They all were in the farming business and were very friendly and kind. Once they knew that I was a farmer's son, they were very eager to show me American farming operations.

I saw and tried all the automated farm equipment, and I saw how they raised cows and pigs, and how they used automatic milking machines, silo towers, and power tools. I was told that the father-and-son team provided all the manpower needed to grow and harvest corn, wheat, and soybeans on the entire five hundred acres of land, and raise cows and pigs. I could not believe how automated and advanced American farming operations were, compared to those in India.

The Thanksgiving dinner table was very nicely set up with many items on the table, including items for vegetarians. There were fourteen family members in attendance. Just like yesterday's dinner, today's special Thanksgiving prayer, formality, discipline, and family traditions were very impressive.

After dinner, we all returned to Danville. That night, they showed me their homemade movies of family activities. I showed my small album and other photos of India. I did not know that anyone could make home movies with a movie camera.

On the Friday after Thanksgiving, the City of Danville had a special reception for all the foreign student guests visiting the city (there were more than twenty of us). The mayor of the city and the council members welcomed all the guests and gave us a tour of the city's operations. After the receptions, the two largest employers in the city—General Motors and Control Devices—gave us guided tours of their local factories. General Motors had large foundry operations, and Control Devices manufactured controls for all types of manufacturing equipment. For me, these tours were interesting because I could relate the factories to my future jobs.

That evening, an Indian doctor named Dr. Majmudar, who was well settled in Danville, invited all the Indian student guests and their hosts for Indian entertainment at his home. His daughter performed a few classical Indian dances, and he played the sitar. His wife served a nice home-cooked Indian dinner. Since leaving India, this was my first occasion to see classical Indian dance and to test Indian food. This made me homesick.

On Saturday morning, Danville High School welcomed all the foreign student guests to the town. After the welcome speech by the principal, all the guests were broken down into small groups. Each group was escorted by a senior student for a guided tour of the high school campus. This was my first visit to an American high school. I was flabbergasted by the facilities the school provided for the students. The classrooms, laboratories, gymnasium, library, auditorium, playground, staff room, first aid room, etc. were well equipped with the latest equipment. Before the end of the visit, the home economics class students served us tasty food samples cooked during the class.

On Saturday afternoon, the plan was to go hunting. I could not tell my host that I do not enjoy hunting. I was prepared to go. But luckily, it snowed heavily during the entire afternoon. The hunting plan was scrapped. Instead, I played card games with the kids. It had been a long time since the last time I'd played card games with kids. I learned new card games and enjoyed them. Later that evening, Dr. and Mrs. Elghammer and I talked about various things about America and India, including the customs, cultures, food, dresses, and many similarities and dissimilarities.

On Sunday morning, I attended a church service with the host family. It was well organized with streamlined events. The audience was very disciplined, courteous, and quiet. The pastor of the church welcomed and thanked all the foreign students in the audience. Later, he also met all guests individually.

After lunch, I packed up to go back to Chicago. Four days of bonding with strangers, excitement, and learning new things were over. The entire Elghammer family came to the railway station to give me a very emotional send-off. The little girl clung to me and said, with tears in her eyes, "Can't you stay a little longer?" The platform was packed with host families and departing foreign students. This created a very emotional atmosphere. This brought sharp memories of me leaving my hometown railway station a few months back.

During this four-day Thanksgiving holiday, I learned a lot about the American family, traditions, religion, culture, farming, and humanity. I experienced the warm side of human beings. This heartwarming experience raised a few questions in my mind about the kind, caring, and welcoming American people. What made them host a foreign student in their house? Was it their religion, love for human beings, or knowing the pain of a foreign student living alone in America? I could not find the answer. Whatever it might have been, the visit was heartwarming.

The trip from Danville to Chicago was sad. I had just left a kind, loving, and caring family, just like I'd left my family in India in August.

14.6 GETTING AMERICAN CITIZENSHIP

I was not sure about getting American citizenship until 1974. Deep down in my mind, I believed that I would someday go back to India and either start a business or work for a top-notch company there. When I visited India in 1974, I visited some of our relatives who had successful businesses. When I saw their business operations, human resources, and management structures, I concluded that running a business in India was not my cup of tea. After making this decision, I talked to a few friends who had gone back to India, worked for companies for a while, and came back to America. They painted a very bleak picture of working in India for American-educated engineers. Manju and I also thought about Neha and Neel. How would they progress in India? Ultimately, I decided not to go back to India. I had a permanent visa (a green card), and there was no reason to hurry to get American citizenship. However, upon the passage of the family reunification law, many Indian green card holders, including Manju, became American citizens and started sponsoring their parents and siblings to get green cards. I did not have any siblings wanting to come to America at that time, except Anjani. Once my siblings had adult kids and found out about the trend, they started putting pressure on me to become an American citizen and sponsor them for receiving a green card. I had no choice but to apply for American citizenship. I was committed to the well-being of my siblings. I collected all the necessary papers; applied for citizenship on January 15, 1980; and received it on April 28, 1980.

Upon receiving American citizenship, I had to let go of my Indian citizenship. It was a tough choice. I was giving up my citizenship of the world's biggest democracy in exchange for the world's strongest democracy.

14.7 THE DAY EMPTYING OUR NEST BEGAN

August 29, 1984, was an important day in our life. It was the beginning of our nest getting empty. Until now we were four living in our nest. It was going to go down to three from this day. Our first child, Neha, was going to start UT(University of Texas) in Austin, TX. Manju and I were going to drop her off at the campus. This was the first time Neha was going to live, in a dorm, away from family and it was also the first time for us that our child moved away from our day-to-day life. It caused a unique pain; one must go through it to understand it.

Our car was loaded with her stuff the previous night. We got up early and got ready to leave. We prayed to Lord Ganesh, other gods and goddesses, and our elders for their blessings before leaving the home. When we sat in the car, I noticed the excitement, worry, and sadness on Neha's face. I was hiding my sadness behind a smiley face. The car ride to Austin was somber, with very little talking.

When we arrived at the campus, we helped her to get dorm keys and then took her stuff to her dorm room. After settling in her room, we helped her identify her daily needs items for dorm living. Took her to a local shopping center and purchased them. We had a late lunch in the dorm cafeteria.

While eating lunch thoughts went through my mind about the dorm cafeteria food. I knew Neha was going to miss her Mama's food. I missed it when I left home for the first time to live in the dorm.

Later that afternoon, Manju and I went to see a local friend and spent the night with them.

Next day morning we came back to her dorm. Walked with her around the UT campus and accompanied her to get her registration and Student ID card. When we returned to her dorm room, we knew the painful moment was coming soon. We sat down with her for last-minute advice and assured her that we loved her and would do anything to support her education.

We walked to our car together. While going to our car, we all were crying. She hugged us, waited till we sat in the car, and then started going back to her dorm. She didn't turn back to see us leaving. We sat in the car for a few minutes till she disappeared, from our sight, into the dorm entrance. We felt that a part of our lives has been separated. For Neha, this was the beginning of a new lifestyle. No more Mom and Dad around to help or watch her.

The return trip, to our home, was even more somber. The sweet memories of seeing her grow from a little girl to a young lady went through our minds and we kept talking about it. We were supposed to stop for lunch on the way from Austin to Plano. We didn't feel like eating.

Our house felt strange when we returned home after dropping her off in Austin, Texas. It looked quiet and empty, even though our family was shrunk by only one member.

For a few days, we felt her absence a lot. Slowly slowly it sank into our minds that she is not with us, for day-to-day life, but for a good purpose. This was a part of life. We must love her and let her go!

14.8 Heart Operation (July 12, 2004)

I consider myself to be a healthy person. I exercise regularly, eat wisely, have normal cholesterol levels and blood pressure, don't have any chest or other pains, abide by a vegetarian diet, and get regular physical examinations and stress tests. Nothing looked abnormal. And suddenly, I failed a regularly scheduled stress test. Everything changed in a flash. My cardiologist called Neha and relayed the bad news. Once Neha saw the stress test results, she grounded me. All the planned trips were canceled. These included the trip I was going to take with Manju for business and pleasure. The trip was scheduled for just a few days after the stress test.

I got an angiography the next day and found out that I had four blocked arteries. I needed to have bypass surgery as soon as possible. I was shaken up. I could not understand. *How did I get to this situation suddenly and without any symptoms?* Luckily, Neel happened to be in town during that time. He assured me that this was normal, that the latest bypass surgery procedures (his field of expertise) were almost 100 percent successful, and that I should not worry about the surgery. The surgery was scheduled for three days after the angiography.

Normally, I am a well-organized person. But this operation surprised me. I had no time to organize my life in case I did not come back home alive. All my family members and friends were shocked and surprised by the news of my heart surgery. No one believed that this could happen to me.

On the day of the surgery, July 12, 2004, we went to Parkland Memorial Hospital in Dallas early in the morning. I was very emotional and completely unable to gather my thoughts. I did not know what to say to Manju, Neha, and Neel. When we arrived at the hospital, we went through the admission process and into the prep area. I bade an emotional goodbye to my family. This could have been the last time they would see me alive. The last thing I remember before the operation was that I was being injected with anesthesia. The operation had a minor glitch of blood leakage after everything was packed back. The leakage required reopening my chest and restitching the artery. This gave a little scare to all the family members.

After the surgery, I was moved to the ICU where I was connected to wires and tubes all over. Late in the afternoon, I started regaining my consciousness intermittently. When I saw and recognized Neha and Anjani were there, the first thing I said was, "I love you all." Manju missed seeing me waking up and hearing my first words. When she came to see me, I was half asleep and did not say anything to her. Other family members and some friends stopped by to see me; I do not remember them.

The first night was difficult and very risky for me. With God's grace and my forefather's blessings, it went by smoothly, and I got my full conscious back.

On the second day, most of the tubes and wires were removed, and I was moved to a regular recovery room. I felt good. The surgery pain was minimal. However, the doctor started the painful rehab process. My lungs collapsed. I had to learn to breathe and open my lungs.

On this day, many local family members and friends came to visit me. I was overwhelmed by their love and wishes for a fast recovery.

The morning of the third day was the worst for my recovery. My stomach was upset, I had a high fever, and I became cranky and grouchy. The nurse forced me to get out of bed and walk a few steps. Later in the day, the fever had subsided, my stomach calmed down, I felt a little better, and I started making progress toward recovery. Also, on this day, many local family members and friends came to visit me.

On the fourth day, I started getting severe pain in my left leg, from where the vein had been removed. On that day, several friends from Texas Instruments came to visit me.

I was supposed to be released from the hospital on the fifth day, but they did not release me, due to the pain in my leg. Otherwise, I felt good and was ready to go home.

On the sixth day, I was supposed to be released in the morning, but my blood pressure had dropped significantly and made me dizzy. After taking the medication, the blood pressure became normal, and I was released in the afternoon. Manju and Neha came to take me home. This was the end of my extended stay in the hospital and the start of my rehab at home. Since my heart was in excellent condition, I did not need any supervised rehab.

Once I came home and news about my heart operation had reached my relatives in India, I got many heartwarming calls from them.

In fourteen days, I felt almost normal. I started walking more than two miles at the Carpenter Recreation Center. I also started taking care of day-to-day business and emails, etc.

The heart operation was the first and most unique hospitalization experience of my life. I recognized and appreciated the loving and caring feelings of my family members and friends. I also recognized and appreciated the work of the hospital workers around the clock.

14.9 LIFETIME ACHIEVEMENTS, REWARDS, AND RECOGNITIONS

The following is a list of all the achievements, rewards, and recognitions—small and big—that I have received during my life so far:

- Received Bhagavad Gita (the most sacred Hindu scripture holy book) from Sheth Nanaji Kalidas, as a prize for being first in the fourth-grade class of Shapur Elementary School in June 1953.
- Received two rupees as a prize from the classroom teacher Mr. Vyas, for being first in the ninth-grade class of the city's middle school in Junagadh in May 1956.
- Passed SSC exam (high school), with distinction, in June 1958.
- Received Professor N. B. Pends Prize (with a prize of three hundred rupees) for getting the highest grades in mathematics in the first year of junior college at Bahauddin College in Junagadh in 1959.

- Received Amrutbai Scholarship for good grades in the first year of junior college in 1959.
- Received merit scholarships from the Government of India and Patel Mohanlal Gokaldas Scholarship Fund for three years in engineering college between 1960 and 1963.
- Received first prize in the technical exhibition for preparing a model of a dam with automatic flood control gates (during the second year of engineering college in 1962).
- Elected class representative of the Bachelor of Engineering-Mechanical class of 1962.
- Received bachelor's degree in mechanical engineering, with first class, in June 1963.
- Received master's degree in mechanical engineering, with honors, in January 1965.
- Received PhD degree in industrial engineering and operations research in June 1974.
- Received professional engineer's (PE) certification in 1979.
- Received certified quality engineer's (CQE) certification in 1983.
- Participated in the formation of the Dallas Indian Lions Club and became a charter member of the club in 1985.
- Received SEMATECH's excellence award for publishing guidelines for equipment reliability in May 1993.
- Became president of the DFW Hindu Temple Society in 1993.
- Published my book, *Hi-Tech Equipment Reliability*, in 1995. Revised it and published the second edition in 2008.
- Became a trustee of the DFW Hindu Temple Society from 1996 to 2002.
- Received senior member of technical staff (SMTS) title at Texas Instruments Inc. in 1996.
- Received fellow of the American Society for Quality (ASQ) recognition in November 1998.
- Authored a section in *Handbook of Semiconductor Manufacturing Technology* in 2000.
- My book, *Hi-Tech Equipment Reliability*, was translated into Japanese and got published in Japan in July 2002.

15

SUMMARY OF THE FACTORS THAT HELPED ME, A TRANSPLANTED MAN, TO THRIVE

I was born in a small town in India and was raised in a large, joint farming family in a very primitive house and living environment. During my childhood, the social and political environments were very harsh, and my parents didn't have money for any luxury items. I experienced the pain of temporarily migrating to another kingdom (country). However, these environments didn't stop me from getting an education. Once the political environment stabilized in India in 1948, I had no problem completing my elementary, middle, and high school education and getting my bachelor's degree in engineering in India.

After my graduation, I was uprooted at the age of twenty-four from my motherland and was transplanted into the promised land of America. It was a painful separation from my motherland, parents, relatives, friends, and home. When I got transplanted, I knew very little about American culture, society, environment, business systems, living styles, money, diet, etc. Also, at that time, I had just enough money for my college fees and living expenses for a year. In the early days, I was not sure how I was going to survive and thrive in the transplanted land.

When I reflect on my life as presented in this book, I think about what helped elevate me from a primitive life in a small village in India to an upper-middle-class life in America. The following is a summary of items that helped me and my life partner to thrive and live a successful, healthy, and happy life in the transplanted land.

The intention here is to summarize and share the information.

A. Family Matters

- Having adventurous, brave, and visionary forefathers who worked hard, with honesty and dignity, and provided flourishing opportunities for their descendants, including me
- Having hardworking, honest, loving, and visionary parents
- Having a father who was persistent in my education
- Getting encouragement, love, and help from caring uncles, aunts, and elder siblings while growing up
- Having an educated, open-minded, complementary, supportive, hardworking, and loving life partner for our journey together through various phases of our lives
- Having enriching and supportive friends throughout my life
- Having smart, goal-oriented, high achiever, disciplined, loving and caring, well settled in their chosen medical profession, and financially well-off children
- Having the capacity and willingness to uplift the living standards of my parents, brother Devraj (and his kids), and all my sisters

B. Personal Deeds

- Without having any artistic skills (like music, acting, etc.) or sports abilities, the only way to elevate from an ordinary farmer's son to a successful engineering professional was through formal education from elementary, middle, and high school education to undergraduate and postgraduate colleges
- Respecting authority and staying within social boundaries
- Being honest with myself and others
- Working hard, smart, and with honesty for optimum reward

- Being open-minded and flexible to adopt other people's ideas that were better than my own
- Being a loyal and dedicated employee and working hard with honesty and dedication, in the best interest of my employers
- Working for top-notch employers with creativity-inspiring employee benefits
- Being conscious of my physical health, including regularly exercising during my student years, and once I started working, using employers' fitness centers for exercising
- Avoiding confrontation with those with whom I did not agree
- Always trying to avoid confronting people
- Not complaining when faced with problems in life; instead, looking for solutions
- Practicing a combination of daily yoga practice and physical exercise for staying in good health
- Eating only vegetarian foods throughout my life
- Being a follower of the Hindu religion
- Learning to have equality for all human beings, irrespective of race, creed, color, or religion, during all occasions, sad and/or happy

C. Money Matters

- Only working hard is not enough to be rich; smart investing of savings is
- Buying a home as soon as possible, and as big as we could afford to buy, in a highly reputable school district and an open-minded neighborhood that is located a comfortable distance from schools, shopping centers, hospitals, and workplaces
- Not borrowing money that would create large debt beyond our earning capacity
- Paying off debts as soon as possible
- Being my own banker for all my financial needs
- Learning earlier in my life that: (i) investments in stocks are higher-risk investments; (ii) on average, stock investments give better returns on the investments over a long time; (iii) there is no

best time to get into the stock market, it is time in the stock market that pays off; (iv) it's wise to invest in large, reputable, and well-known companies' stocks and/or three index funds (DIA, QQQ, and SPY); (v) one should never buy stocks on margin (borrowing money from the broker to buy stocks); and (vi) one should use big, nationally known, reputable stockbrokers with online trading facilities and financial research

- Also, learning the lesson that nobody will make money for me; I must make money for myself and not fall into the traps of swindling artists

- Believing that, if I want to be rich, then being greedy and saving a small amount is not an efficient way to be rich; looking for ways to earn more from my job, business, and/or investments is a more efficient way

- Taking advantage of employers' incentive plans, such as 401(k) and stock purchase plans

- Regularly saving in the income tax favored plans, such as regular IRAs, Roth IRAs, and 401(k)s.

- Contributing to 529 college saving plans for my young kids and grandkids to encourage them to get a college education

- Giving money to deserving relatives, friends, individuals, and organizations, and not expecting anything in return from the recipients; ignoring any dissatisfaction some of them might have; and considering ourselves fortunate for having the capacity and willingness to support them.

16

PASSING LEGACY

In a few years, I will be gone from this world. I have shared my life story in this book. Now my grandchildren and the future generations will know about their roots and their ancestors who came to America. From where did he come to America? How much did he struggle to establish roots and thrive in the promised land of America?

My life partner and I consider ourselves fortunate to thrive and have a successful and self-satisfying life in the transplanted land. We wish that every transplanted man and woman would thrive, just like us, in the promised land of America, in whatever profession he/she chooses.

This book presents a proven road map for newly transplanted people on how to establish roots in a new country and thrive. If a transplanted man/woman wants to write his/her life story, this book also presents a structural format to write it.

Thank you for reading this book. With best wishes for success in all the endeavors you may seek in the transplanted land. Do not forget to preserve your legacy!

Printed in the United States
by Baker & Taylor Publisher Services